Adelaide Travel Guide 2025

Discover South Australia's Best Attractions, Cultural Experiences, and Outdoor Escapes

Daniel Roger

Copyright

Copyright © 2025 Daniel Roger

All rights reserved. No part of this publication may be reproduced, distributed, or transmitted in any form or by any means, including photocopying, recording, or other electronic or mechanical methods, without the prior written permission of the publisher, except in the case of brief quotations embodied in critical reviews and certain other noncommercial uses permitted by copyright law.

About the Author

Daniel Roger is a seasoned traveler, explorer, and storyteller with a passion for uncovering the world's most breathtaking landscapes and hidden treasures. With years of experience navigating remote destinations, bustling cities, and cultural heartlands, Daniel has developed a keen eye for detail and an innate ability to bring places to life through vivid storytelling and expert travel insights.

From towering mountain ranges to vibrant coastal communities, his journeys are driven by a deep curiosity for the world's diverse cultures, natural wonders, and untamed wilderness. With a knack for practical travel advice and a love for immersive experiences, Daniel empowers adventurers—whether first-time explorers or seasoned globetrotters—to step off the beaten path and embrace the extraordinary.

Blending meticulous research with firsthand experience, Daniel's writing is more than just a guide—it's an invitation to embark on unforgettable journeys with confidence and curiosity. His mission is simple: to inspire, inform, and equip travelers with everything they need to create their own remarkable adventures.

Table of Contents

1. Introduction to Adelaide 1
History: 2
Climate: 6
2. Getting to Adelaide 9
By Air: 9
By Train: 9
By Bus: 10
By Car: 12
3. Getting Around Adelaide 15
Public Transportation: 15
Cycling: 16
Car Rental: 17
4. Accommodation 21
Hotels: 21
Bed and Breakfasts: 23
Hostels: 26
5. Dining and Cuisine 33
Local Specialties: 33
Restaurants: 35
Cafes: 37
Food Markets: 40
6. Attractions in Adelaide 45
Adelaide Botanic Garden: 45
Adelaide Zoo: 45

Adelaide Central Market: 45
Adelaide Oval: 46
Art Gallery of South Australia: 46
Adelaide Hills: 47

7. Cultural Experiences 51
Festivals and Events: 51
Theatres and Performing Arts: 53
Museums and Galleries: 56
Aboriginal Culture Experiences: 58

8. Outdoor Activities 63
Hiking and Bushwalking: 63
Cycling Trails: 65
Water Sports (Sailing, Kayaking, Surfing): 68
Golf Courses: 70
2. Kooyonga Golf Club: 71
Wildlife Watching: 73

9. Shopping 77
Rundle Mall: 77
Boutique Stores: 79
Souvenir Shops: 81
Local Markets: 83

10. Nightlife and Entertainment 87
Bars and Pubs: 87
Nightclubs: 89

    Live Music Venues: 91
    Theatre Shows: 94
11. Day Trips and Excursions 97
    McLaren Vale Wine Region: 97
    Adelaide Hills Wineries: 99
    Kangaroo Island: 101
    Fleurieu Peninsula: 103
    Murray River Cruises: 105
12. Practical Information 111
13. Travel Tips 113
14. Resources 115
Map 117

1. Introduction to Adelaide

Adelaide, the capital city of South Australia, is a charming blend of natural beauty, cultural richness, and urban sophistication. Situated on the southern coast of Australia, Adelaide is renowned for its well-planned layout, expansive parklands, and vibrant arts scene. With a population of around 1.3 million people, it strikes a balance between a bustling city atmosphere and a relaxed lifestyle.

One of Adelaide's distinctive features is its grid-like layout, with wide streets and spacious squares, making it easy to navigate and explore. The city is flanked by the picturesque Mount Lofty Ranges to the east and the pristine beaches of the Gulf St Vincent to the west, offering residents and visitors alike a diverse range of outdoor activities and scenic vistas.

Adelaide has a rich cultural heritage, evident in its historic architecture, thriving arts scene, and multicultural population. From the bustling Central Market to the iconic

Adelaide Oval, the city is home to a wealth of attractions and landmarks that showcase its unique character and charm.

With a Mediterranean climate, Adelaide enjoys long, sunny days and mild winters, making it an ideal destination year-round. Whether you're strolling along the vibrant streets of the city center, sampling world-class wines in the nearby Barossa Valley, or soaking up the sun on the sandy shores of Glenelg Beach, Adelaide offers something for everyone to enjoy.

In this guide, we'll delve deeper into the wonders of Adelaide, exploring its attractions, dining scene, cultural experiences, outdoor activities, and more, to help you make the most of your visit to this vibrant South Australian city. Welcome to Adelaide – where culture, nature, and urban charm converge.

History:

Adelaide's history is a tapestry woven with the threads of Indigenous heritage, colonial settlement, and cultural evolution. The city's story begins long before European arrival, with the Indigenous Kaurna people as the traditional custodians of the land.

- **Indigenous Heritage**: The Kaurna people have inhabited the Adelaide Plains for tens of thousands of years, living in harmony with the natural environment and establishing a rich cultural legacy. Their connection to the land is evident in the numerous Dreaming stories and cultural sites scattered throughout the region.

- **Colonial Settlement**: In 1836, Adelaide was founded as a planned colony by Colonel William Light, a British surveyor-general. His vision for the city was one of wide boulevards, expansive parklands, and a layout designed for both beauty and functionality. Adelaide was intended to be a free settlement, in contrast to the penal colonies established elsewhere in Australia, attracting migrants seeking a new start and opportunities for prosperity.

- **Early Growth and Development**: The early years of Adelaide were marked by rapid growth and development, fueled by immigration, agricultural expansion, and the discovery of mineral resources. The city became a hub for trade and commerce, with bustling markets, thriving industries, and a burgeoning cultural scene.

- **Cultural Diversity**: Adelaide's cultural landscape was enriched by successive waves of immigration from around the world, including European settlers, Chinese immigrants, and later, refugees from war-torn countries. This diversity is reflected in the city's architecture, cuisine, and traditions, creating a vibrant tapestry of cultural expression.

- **Modern Era**: In the 20th and 21st centuries, Adelaide continued to evolve and adapt to changing economic and social dynamics. The city embraced innovation and technology, becoming a center for research, education, and healthcare. Today, Adelaide is renowned for its high quality of life, cultural vibrancy, and forward-thinking mindset.

As we explore Adelaide's history, we gain a deeper understanding of the forces that have shaped the city and its people, from ancient times to the present day. Through its triumphs and challenges, Adelaide remains a testament to the resilience, creativity, and spirit of its inhabitants.

Geography:

Adelaide's geography is characterized by a captivating blend of coastal beauty, rolling hills, and fertile plains, providing a stunning backdrop for the city's vibrant urban landscape. Situated in the south of Australia, Adelaide is the capital city of the state of South Australia and is strategically located between the Gulf St Vincent to the west and the Mount Lofty Ranges to the east.

- **Coastline**: Adelaide's western boundary is defined by the azure waters of the Gulf St Vincent, offering residents and visitors alike access to pristine beaches, tranquil bays, and picturesque coastal scenery. Popular seaside destinations such as Glenelg, Semaphore, and Henley Beach are beloved for their sandy shores, vibrant esplanades, and array of recreational activities.

- **Mount Lofty Ranges**: To the east of the city lies the Mount Lofty Ranges, a series of rolling hills and verdant valleys that provide a stunning natural backdrop to the urban landscape. Mount Lofty itself, the highest peak in the ranges, offers panoramic views of Adelaide and the surrounding countryside, making it a popular destination for hikers and nature enthusiasts.

- **Adelaide Plains**: Nestled between the Gulf St Vincent and the Mount Lofty Ranges lies the Adelaide Plains, a fertile expanse of land that forms the heartland of the city. The plains are home to lush vineyards, verdant parklands, and vibrant urban neighborhoods, making them an integral part of Adelaide's identity and character.

- **Parklands**: One of Adelaide's most distinctive features is its expansive parklands, which encircle the city center and provide a green oasis amid the urban landscape. The Adelaide Park Lands comprise over 700 hectares of open space, including botanical gardens, recreational reserves, and sporting facilities, offering residents and visitors alike a tranquil retreat from the hustle and bustle of city life.

- **Climate**: Adelaide enjoys a Mediterranean climate, characterized by hot, dry summers and cool, wet winters.

The city experiences relatively mild temperatures year-round, with an average of over 3,000 hours of sunshine annually. This temperate climate makes Adelaide an ideal destination for outdoor activities, festivals, and al fresco dining throughout the year.

As we explore Adelaide's geography, we discover a city blessed with natural beauty, diverse landscapes, and a unique blend of coastal and inland charm. From its sandy beaches to its lush hillsides, Adelaide offers a wealth of opportunities for exploration, adventure, and appreciation of the natural world.

Climate:

Adelaide enjoys a Mediterranean climate, characterized by long, warm summers and mild, wet winters. This climate pattern is influenced by its coastal location along the Gulf St Vincent and its proximity to the Mount Lofty Ranges. The city experiences distinct seasons, each offering its own unique charms and opportunities for outdoor activities.

- **Summer (December - February):** Adelaide's summers are typically hot and dry, with temperatures often reaching into the high 30s Celsius (around 90-100°F). Sea breezes from the Gulf St Vincent provide some relief from the heat, especially in coastal areas. Summer is the perfect time to enjoy the city's beaches, outdoor festivals, and alfresco dining.

- **Autumn (March - May):** Autumn in Adelaide brings mild temperatures and clear skies, making it an ideal season for exploring the city's parks, gardens, and vineyards. The changing colors of the leaves in the Adelaide

Hills create a picturesque backdrop for hiking, cycling, and wine tasting.

- Winter (June - August): Adelaide's winters are cool and wet, with occasional frosts in the hills and suburbs. Average temperatures range from 8-16°C (46-61°F), making it the coldest time of year. Despite the cooler weather, winter is still a great time to explore Adelaide's cultural attractions, cozy cafes, and indoor markets.

- Spring (September - November): Spring heralds the arrival of warmer temperatures and blooming flowers, signaling the start of outdoor festivities and events. Average temperatures range from 12-22°C (54-72°F), making it a pleasant season for outdoor activities such as hiking, cycling, and picnicking in the parklands.

Throughout the year, Adelaide benefits from an abundance of sunshine, with over 2,800 hours of sunshine annually. This sunny climate contributes to the city's vibrant outdoor lifestyle, with residents and visitors alike taking advantage of the countless opportunities for outdoor recreation and relaxation.

While Adelaide's climate is generally mild and temperate, it's always a good idea to check the weather forecast before planning outdoor activities, especially during the summer months when temperatures can soar. With its Mediterranean climate and four distinct seasons, Adelaide offers a year-round destination for travelers seeking sun, sea, and outdoor adventure.

2. Getting to Adelaide

By Air:

Adelaide is serviced by Adelaide Airport (ADL), located approximately 6 kilometers west of the city center. As one of Australia's major airports, Adelaide Airport offers domestic and international flights, providing convenient access to the city for travelers from around the world.

- **Domestic Flights**: Domestic airlines such as Qantas, Virgin Australia, Jetstar, and Rex operate frequent flights to Adelaide from major cities across Australia, including Sydney, Melbourne, Brisbane, Perth, and Darwin. Flight durations vary depending on the origin city, with direct flights typically ranging from 1 to 3 hours.

- **International Flights**: Adelaide Airport also serves as a gateway to South Australia for international travelers, with direct flights available from select destinations in Asia, Oceania, and the Middle East. Airlines such as Singapore Airlines, Cathay Pacific, Qatar Airways, and Air New Zealand offer international flights to Adelaide, connecting the city to global hubs such as Singapore, Hong Kong, Doha, and Auckland.

Upon arrival at Adelaide Airport, travelers can easily access the city center via various transportation options, including taxis, ride sharing services, shuttle buses, and public transportation (bus and tram).

By Train:

Traveling to Adelaide by train offers a scenic and leisurely way to experience the beauty of Australia's landscapes, with comfortable rail services connecting the city to neighboring states and regions.

- **The Ghan**: Operated by Great Southern Rail, The Ghan is an iconic train journey that traverses the heart of Australia from Adelaide to Darwin, spanning over 2,979 kilometers and showcasing the diverse landscapes of the outback. The journey takes approximately 54 hours, with stops at key destinations along the way, including Alice Springs and Katherine.

- **Indian Pacific**: Another renowned train service operated by Great Southern Rail, the Indian Pacific travels between Sydney and Perth, passing through Adelaide on its transcontinental journey. The trip covers a distance of 4,352 kilometers and takes around 65 hours, offering passengers breathtaking views of the Nullarbor Plain, Flinders Ranges, and other iconic landmarks.

In addition to these long-distance train services, Adelaide is also connected to regional towns and cities within South Australia via the South Australian Railways network. The Adelaide Railway Station, located in the heart of the city, serves as a central transportation hub for both interstate and intrastate train services.

Travelers arriving by train can easily access the city center from Adelaide Railway Station via taxi, ride-sharing services, or public transportation (bus and tram), with various accommodation options available nearby for added convenience.

By Bus:

Traveling to Adelaide by bus offers a cost-effective and convenient option for those seeking to explore South Australia and its neighboring states by road. Several bus companies operate services to and from Adelaide, providing connections to major cities, regional towns, and tourist destinations.

- **Interstate Bus Services**: Companies such as Greyhound Australia, Premier Stateliner, and Firefly Express operate interstate bus services that connect Adelaide to cities and towns across Australia, including Melbourne, Sydney, Brisbane, and Perth. These services offer comfortable coaches equipped with amenities such as reclining seats, air conditioning, and onboard entertainment, making long-distance travel a breeze.

- **Regional Bus Services**: Within South Australia, various regional bus operators provide connections between Adelaide and surrounding towns and regions. These services offer an affordable and flexible way to explore the state's diverse landscapes, from the scenic Adelaide Hills to the picturesque Fleurieu Peninsula and beyond.

- **Airport Shuttle Services**: Adelaide Airport offers shuttle bus services that transport passengers between the airport and the city center, as well as other key locations such as Glenelg and the Adelaide Hills. These services operate at regular intervals throughout the day and provide a convenient option for travelers arriving or departing by air.

Travelers arriving by bus can easily access the city center from the Adelaide Central Bus Station, located on Franklin Street in the heart of the CBD. From there, they can utilize various transportation options such as taxis, ride-sharing services, or public transportation (bus and tram) to reach their final destination or accommodation.

By Car:

Driving to Adelaide offers flexibility and freedom to explore the city and its surrounding regions at your own pace, with well-maintained road networks providing easy access from all directions.

- **Major Highways:** Adelaide is connected to other major cities and regions via a network of highways and major roads, including the National Highway network. The South Eastern Freeway connects Adelaide to Melbourne in the east, while the Princes Highway links Adelaide to Sydney via the scenic coastal route. The Eyre Highway provides access to Perth and Western Australia to the west, while the Stuart Highway connects Adelaide to Alice Springs and Darwin in the north.

- **Car Rental:** Rental car companies operate at Adelaide Airport and various locations throughout the city, offering a wide range of vehicles to suit different preferences and budgets. Renting a car provides the flexibility to explore Adelaide and its surrounding regions independently, from the picturesque Adelaide Hills to the renowned wine regions of the Barossa Valley and McLaren Vale.

- **Parking:** Adelaide offers ample parking options for drivers, including metered street parking, multi-level car parks, and designated parking areas at popular attractions and destinations. It's important to familiarize yourself with parking regulations and fees, particularly in the city center where parking restrictions may apply.

Whether you're arriving from interstate or embarking on a road trip within South Australia, traveling to Adelaide by bus or car provides a convenient and flexible way to experience the city and its diverse surroundings, from coastal landscapes to rolling hills and beyond.

3. Getting Around Adelaide

Public Transportation:

Adelaide offers a comprehensive public transportation network that provides convenient and affordable options for getting around the city and its surrounding regions. From buses and trams to trains, Adelaide's public transport system makes it easy to explore the city's attractions, suburbs, and beyond.

- **Adelaide Metro**: Adelaide Metro operates the city's public transport services, including buses, trams, and trains. The network covers the Adelaide metropolitan area and extends to some regional areas within South Australia.

    - **Buses:** Adelaide Metro buses operate on a comprehensive network of routes, providing access to key destinations throughout the city and suburbs. Services run regularly, with frequent stops and connections available at major transport interchanges.

    - **Trams**: The Adelaide tram network, known as the Glenelg tram line, operates between the Adelaide CBD and the beachside suburb of Glenelg. The tramline offers a convenient and scenic way to travel between the city and the coast, with stops at popular attractions along the route.

    - **Trains**: Adelaide Metro trains operate on several suburban and intercity rail lines, providing connections to destinations within the metropolitan area and beyond. Services run regularly throughout the day, with stations located at key transport hubs and popular destinations.

- **Ticketing**: Adelaide Metro offers a range of ticketing options, including single trip tickets, day passes, and multi-trip tickets (MetroCard). Passengers can purchase tickets from ticket vending machines located at train stations, tram stops, and selected retailers, or use the MetroCard for convenient tap-on, tap-off travel.

- **Accessibility**: Adelaide Metro is committed to providing accessible transportation for all passengers, with low-floor buses, tram stops, and train stations equipped with ramps, elevators, and other accessibility features to accommodate passengers with mobility needs.

Cycling:

Cycling is a popular and eco-friendly way to explore Adelaide, with a network of dedicated bike paths, lanes, and trails providing safe and scenic routes for cyclists of all abilities. From leisurely rides along the River Torrens Linear Park Trail to challenging mountain bike trails in the Adelaide Hills, there's something for every cyclist to enjoy in Adelaide.

- **Bike Hire**: Visitors can rent bicycles from various bike hire shops and rental companies located throughout the city, offering a range of bikes to suit different preferences and skill levels. Many hotels and hostels also offer bike rental services for guests.

- **Bike Paths and Trails**: Adelaide boasts a network of well-maintained bike paths and trails that traverse the city and its surrounding regions, offering cyclists the opportunity to explore scenic landscapes, parks, and attractions. Popular routes include the River Torrens

Linear Park Trail, the Coast to Vines Rail Trail, and the Mike Turtur Bikeway.

- **Cycling Infrastructure**: Adelaide is committed to promoting cycling as a sustainable mode of transportation, with dedicated bike lanes, shared paths, and bike-friendly infrastructure integrated into the city's urban planning and development. Cyclists can enjoy safe and convenient access to key destinations, including the city center, beaches, and parklands.

- **Safety Tips:** Cyclists are encouraged to observe road rules and safety guidelines when riding in Adelaide, including wearing a helmet, using lights and reflective gear at night, and signaling when turning or changing lanes. It's also important to be aware of other road users and to ride defensively to ensure a safe and enjoyable cycling experience.

Whether you choose to explore Adelaide by public transportation or bicycle, you'll find a range of convenient and sustainable options for getting around the city and experiencing its diverse attractions, landscapes, and culture.

Car Rental:

Renting a car in Adelaide provides travelers with the flexibility and freedom to explore the city and its surrounding regions at their own pace. With a range of rental car companies operating in Adelaide, visitors can choose from a variety of vehicles to suit their preferences and travel needs.

- **Rental Companies**: Major car rental companies such as Avis, Budget, Hertz, Thrifty, and Europcar operate at

Adelaide Airport and various locations throughout the city. These companies offer a wide selection of vehicles, including economy cars, sedans, SUVs, and luxury vehicles, allowing travelers to choose the perfect car for their journey.

- **Booking:** Travelers can easily book a rental car in advance through the rental company's website or by contacting their customer service hotline. Booking in advance ensures availability and allows travelers to compare prices, vehicle options, and rental terms to find the best deal for their budget and itinerary.

- **Pick-Up and Drop-Off**: Rental cars can be picked up and returned at Adelaide Airport, downtown locations, or other designated rental depots. Most rental companies offer flexible pick-up and drop-off times, allowing travelers to schedule their rental period according to their travel plans.

- **Driving in Adelaide**: Adelaide's road network is well-maintained and easy to navigate, with clear signage and well-marked roads. Driving in the city center can be busy during peak hours, but traffic generally flows smoothly outside of rush periods. Visitors should familiarize themselves with local road rules and regulations, including speed limits, parking restrictions, and driving etiquette.

- **Parking**: Adelaide offers ample parking options for drivers, including metered street parking, multi-level car parks, and designated parking areas at popular attractions and destinations. Visitors should be mindful of parking regulations and fees, particularly in the city center where parking restrictions may apply.

Walking Tours:

Exploring Adelaide on foot is a delightful way to immerse yourself in the city's rich history, vibrant culture, and scenic beauty. Whether you're wandering through historic neighborhoods, strolling along the riverbank, or discovering hidden gems in the city center, Adelaide offers a wealth of walking tours and self-guided walking routes to suit every interest and itinerary.

- **Guided Tours**: Numerous tour operators in Adelaide offer guided walking tours that explore various aspects of the city, from its colonial heritage and architectural landmarks to its culinary delights and hidden alleyways. Guided tours are led by knowledgeable local guides who provide fascinating insights and anecdotes along the way.

- **Self-Guided Tours**: For independent travelers, self-guided walking tours offer the flexibility to explore Adelaide at your own pace and on your own schedule. Visitors can download walking tour maps and audio guides from tourism websites or pick up printed guides from visitor information centers, allowing them to discover Adelaide's attractions and landmarks at their leisure.

- **Popular Walking Routes**: Some of Adelaide's most popular walking routes include the Adelaide Park Lands Trail, which circumnavigates the city center through expansive parklands and gardens, and the Adelaide City Heritage Trail, which showcases the city's historic buildings and cultural landmarks. Other scenic routes include the River Torrens Linear Park Trail, the North Terrace Cultural Boulevard, and the Glenelg Foreshore Promenade.

- **Safety Tips:** When embarking on a walking tour in Adelaide, it's important to wear comfortable footwear, dress appropriately for the weather, and stay hydrated. Be mindful of traffic and pedestrian crossings, especially when walking in busy areas or crossing streets. It's also a good idea to carry a map, guidebook, or smartphone with GPS to help navigate your route and discover points of interest along the way.

Whether you're exploring Adelaide by rental car or on foot, you'll find a variety of convenient and enjoyable ways to discover the city's attractions, landscapes, and culture. From scenic drives through the Adelaide Hills to leisurely strolls along the riverbank, Adelaide offers endless opportunities for exploration and adventure.

4. Accommodation

Hotels:

Adelaide offers a diverse range of hotels to suit every budget, preference, and travel style. From luxurious five-star properties to boutique hotels and budget-friendly accommodations, visitors can choose from a variety of options conveniently located in the city center and surrounding suburbs.

1. InterContinental Adelaide
   - Website: [InterContinental Adelaide] (https://www.ihg.com/intercontinental/hotels/us/en/adelaide/adelc/hoteldetail)
   - Description: Located on the picturesque North Terrace overlooking the River Torrens, InterContinental Adelaide offers elegant rooms, upscale dining options, and luxurious amenities for discerning travelers.

2. Hilton Adelaide
   - Website: [Hilton Adelaide] (https://www.hilton.com/en/hotels/adlhthi-hilton-adelaide/)
   - Description: Situated in the heart of the CBD, Hilton Adelaide boasts stylish accommodations, award-winning restaurants, and state-of-the-art facilities, including a rooftop swimming pool and fitness center.

3. Mayfair Hotel Adelaide
   - Website: [Mayfair Hotel Adelaide] (https://www.mayfairhotel.com.au/)
   - Description: Housed in a beautifully restored heritage building, Mayfair Hotel Adelaide offers boutique luxury

accommodations, personalized service, and a range of dining and entertainment options in a prime city location.

4. Oaks Adelaide Embassy Suites
   - Website: [Oaks Adelaide Embassy Suites] (https://www.oakshotels.com/en/oaks-adelaide-embassy-suites)
      - Description: Located adjacent to the Adelaide Convention Centre, Oaks Adelaide Embassy Suites offers contemporary apartment-style accommodations with fully equipped kitchens, separate living areas, and stunning city views.

5. Adina Apartment Hotel Adelaide Treasury
   - Website: [Adina Apartment Hotel Adelaide Treasury] (https://www.adinahotels.com/en/apartments/adelaide-treasury/)
      - Description: Set within a historic former treasury building, Adina Apartment Hotel Adelaide Treasury offers spacious self-contained apartments, modern amenities, and a central location near Rundle Mall and Adelaide's cultural attractions.

6. ibis Adelaide
   - Website: [ibis Adelaide] (https://www.accorhotels.com/gb/hotel-8822-ibis-adelaide/index.shtml)
      - Description: Offering comfortable and affordable accommodations in the heart of the CBD, ibis Adelaide provides modern rooms, a 24-hour fitness center, and convenient access to shopping, dining, and entertainment options.

7. Stamford Plaza Adelaide
   - Website: [Stamford Plaza Adelaide] (https://www.stamford.com.au/spa)

- Description: Boasting panoramic views of the Adelaide Oval and River Torrens, Stamford Plaza Adelaide offers luxurious accommodations, fine dining experiences, and impeccable service in a prime location near the city's top attractions.

8. Holiday Inn Express Adelaide City Centre
   - Website: [Holiday Inn Express Adelaide City Centre](https://www.ihg.com/holidayinnexpress/hotels/us/en/adelaide/adlcc/hoteldetail)
   - Description: Providing comfortable and affordable accommodations for both business and leisure travelers, Holiday Inn Express Adelaide City Centre offers modern rooms, complimentary breakfast, and a central location close to major landmarks and transport hubs.

These hotels represent just a sample of the wide range of accommodations available in Adelaide. Visitors can explore additional options on booking platforms such as Booking.com, Expedia, or directly through the hotel websites for the most up-to-date availability and rates.

Bed and Breakfasts:

For travelers seeking a more intimate and personalized lodging experience, bed and breakfasts in Adelaide offer charm, hospitality, and a homely atmosphere. From historic cottages to elegant guesthouses, these B&Bs provide comfortable accommodations, delicious breakfasts, and a warm welcome from friendly hosts.

1. Adelaide Heritage Cottages & Apartments
   - Website: [Adelaide Heritage Cottages & Apartments](https://adelaideheritage.com/)

- Description: Located in the leafy suburb of North Adelaide, Adelaide Heritage Cottages & Apartments offers a range of heritage-style accommodations, including self-contained cottages and apartments with modern amenities and tranquil garden settings.

2. Adelaide Travellers Inn Backpackers Hostel & B&B

   - Website: [Adelaide Travellers Inn Backpackers Hostel & B&B](https://www.adelaidetravellersinn.com.au/)
   - Description: Situated in the vibrant East End of Adelaide's CBD, Adelaide Travellers Inn Backpackers Hostel & B&B offers affordable and comfortable accommodations for budget-conscious travelers, with both dormitory-style rooms and private ensuite rooms available.

3. Aldgate Lodge Bed and Breakfast

   - Website: [Aldgate Lodge Bed and Breakfast](https://www.aldgatelodge.com.au/)
   - Description: Nestled in the picturesque Adelaide Hills town of Aldgate, Aldgate Lodge Bed and Breakfast offers cozy and welcoming accommodations in a tranquil garden setting, with hearty breakfasts and warm hospitality from the hosts.

4. Bellevue Bed & Breakfast

   - Website: [Bellevue Bed & Breakfast](http://www.bellevuebnb.com.au/)
   - Description: Set in a charming Victorian-era house in the historic suburb of Glenelg, Bellevue Bed & Breakfast offers elegant and spacious guest rooms, gourmet breakfasts, and personalized service just steps away from the beach and Jetty Road precinct.

5. Fire Station Inn
   - Website: [Fire Station Inn](https://www.firestationinn.com.au/)
   - Description: Housed in a beautifully restored fire station in the heart of North Adelaide, Fire Station Inn offers unique and luxurious accommodations in themed suites featuring original fire station memorabilia, spa baths, and private courtyards.

6. Adelaide's Brownhill Creek Caravan and Holiday Park
   - Website: [Adelaide's Brownhill Creek Caravan and Holiday Park](https://www.brownhillcreekcaravanpark.com.au/)
   - Description: Located just 7 kilometers from the Adelaide CBD, Adelaide's Brownhill Creek Caravan and Holiday Park offers a range of accommodation options, including powered sites for caravans, cabins, and self-contained units amidst natural bushland surrounds.

7. Athelney Cottage Bed and Breakfast
   - Website: [Athelney Cottage Bed and Breakfast](https://www.athelneycottage.com.au/)
   - Description: Tucked away in the tranquil Adelaide Hills village of Stirling, Athelney Cottage Bed and Breakfast offers cozy and romantic accommodations in a heritage-listed cottage surrounded by beautiful gardens and scenic views.

8. Adelaide Hills Retreats
   - Website: [Adelaide Hills Retreats](https://adelaidehillsretreats.com.au/)
   - Description: Providing a selection of luxurious self-contained cottages and suites in the picturesque Adelaide Hills, Adelaide Hills Retreats offers a peaceful retreat with

modern amenities, spa baths, and panoramic views of the surrounding countryside.

These bed and breakfasts offer a warm welcome and a home away from home for travelers seeking a unique and memorable stay in Adelaide. Guests can book directly through the property websites or contact the hosts for more information about availability, rates, and special packages.

Hostels:

For budget-conscious travelers and backpackers, hostels in Adelaide offer affordable accommodations, a friendly atmosphere, and the opportunity to meet fellow travelers from around the world. With convenient locations, shared facilities, and a range of room options, hostels provide a comfortable and social environment for exploring the city and its attractions.

1. Adelaide Central YHA
   - Website: [Adelaide Central YHA] (https://www.yha.com.au/hostels/sa/adelaide/adelaide-central-backpackers-hostel/)
   - Description: Located in the heart of Adelaide's CBD, Adelaide Central YHA offers affordable dormitory and private rooms, communal kitchen and lounge areas, and a rooftop terrace with panoramic views of the city skyline.

2. Backpack Oz
   - Website: [Backpack Oz] (https://www.backpackoz.com.au/)
   - Description: Situated in the vibrant East End of Adelaide's CBD, Backpack Oz offers budget-friendly accommodation options including dormitory beds and

private rooms, as well as a lively onsite bar, communal kitchen, and social events.

3. Shakespeare Backpackers International Hostel
   - Website: [Shakespeare Backpackers International Hostel](https://shakespearebackpackers.com.au/)
   - Description: Located just a short walk from Adelaide's Central Market and Chinatown, Shakespeare Backpackers International Hostel offers affordable accommodations in dormitory-style rooms, with shared kitchen facilities and a communal lounge area.

4. Glenelg Beach Hostel
   - Website: [Glenelg Beach Hostel](https://glenelgbeachhostel.com.au/)
   - Description: Situated in the popular beachside suburb of Glenelg, Glenelg Beach Hostel offers budget-friendly accommodations just steps away from the sand and surf, with dormitory beds and private rooms available and a lively atmosphere.

5. Adelaide Travellers Inn Backpackers Hostel & B&B
   - Website: [Adelaide Travellers Inn Backpackers Hostel & B&B](https://www.adelaidetravellersinn.com.au/)
   - Description: Located in the vibrant East End of Adelaide's CBD, Adelaide Travellers Inn Backpackers Hostel & B&B offers affordable accommodations for budget-conscious travelers, with dormitory beds and private ensuite rooms available.

6. Blue Galah International Backpackers Hostel
   - Website: [Blue Galah International Backpackers Hostel](https://www.bluegalah.com.au/)

- Description: Situated in the heart of Adelaide's CBD, Blue Galah International Backpackers Hostel offers budget-friendly accommodations with a laid-back atmosphere, communal kitchen facilities, and regular social events and activities.

7. My Place & Adelaide Backpackers Hostel
   - Website: [My Place & Adelaide Backpackers Hostel](https://www.myplacebackpackers.com.au/)
   - Description: Located in the West End of Adelaide's CBD, My Place & Adelaide Backpackers Hostel offers affordable accommodations in a historic building with dormitory beds and private rooms, communal kitchen facilities, and a cozy lounge area.

8. Hostel 109 Flashpackers
   - Website: [Hostel 109 Flashpackers](https://www.hostel109.com/)
   - Description: Situated in the vibrant East End of Adelaide's CBD, Hostel 109 Flashpackers offers modern and stylish accommodations with dormitory beds and private rooms, as well as a rooftop terrace, communal kitchen, and onsite cafe.

These hostels provide budget-friendly accommodations and a welcoming atmosphere for travelers looking to explore Adelaide on a shoestring budget. Guests can book directly through the hostel websites or contact the properties for more information about availability, rates, and special offers.

Vacation Rentals:

Vacation rentals in Adelaide offer travelers the opportunity to enjoy a home-away-from-home experience, with the privacy, comfort, and flexibility of self-contained accommodations. From cozy apartments and townhouses to spacious villas and holiday homes, vacation rentals provide a range of options for families, groups, and solo travelers alike.

1. Airbnb
   - Website: [Airbnb - Adelaide] (https://www.airbnb.com/s/Adelaide--Australia)
   - Description: Airbnb offers a wide selection of vacation rentals in Adelaide, including apartments, houses, cottages, and unique properties hosted by local hosts. Guests can choose from a variety of listings based on location, amenities, and budget preferences.

2. Stayz
   - Website: [Stayz - Adelaide] (https://www.stayz.com.au/accommodation/sa/adelaide)
   - Description: Stayz features a range of holiday homes, apartments, and vacation rentals in Adelaide and its surrounding regions, providing travelers with a diverse selection of accommodations to suit their needs and preferences.

3. Booking.com Vacation Rentals
   - Website: [Booking.com Vacation Rentals - Adelaide](https://www.booking.com/vacation-rentals/city/au/adelaide.en-gb.html)
   - Description: Booking.com offers a variety of vacation rentals in Adelaide, including apartments, villas, holiday homes, and serviced apartments, with options available for every budget and travel style.

4. HomeAway
   - Website: [HomeAway - Adelaide] (https://www.homeaway.com.au/holiday-rentals/australia/adelaide-region)

- Description: HomeAway features a range of holiday rentals and vacation homes in Adelaide and its surrounding regions, allowing guests to enjoy the comforts of home while exploring the city's attractions and landmarks.

5. TripAdvisor Vacation Rentals
   - Website: [TripAdvisor Vacation Rentals - Adelaide] (https://www.tripadvisor.com/VacationRentals-g255093-Reviews-Adelaide_Greater_Adelaide_South_Australia-Vacation_Rentals.html)
   - Description: TripAdvisor offers a selection of vacation rentals in Adelaide, including apartments, cottages, and holiday homes, with user reviews and ratings to help travelers find the perfect accommodation for their trip.

6. Vrbo
   - Website: [Vrbo - Adelaide] (https://www.vrbo.com/vacation-rentals/australia/adelaide)
   - Description: Vrbo features a range of vacation rentals in Adelaide, including apartments, houses, and holiday homes, providing guests with a comfortable and convenient base for exploring the city and its surroundings.

7. FlipKey
   - Website: [FlipKey - Adelaide] (https://www.flipkey.com/book/adelaide/222366791/)
   - Description: FlipKey offers vacation rentals in Adelaide, including apartments, villas, and holiday homes, with amenities such as fully equipped kitchens, laundry facilities, and outdoor spaces for relaxation and enjoyment.

8. HometoGo

- Website: [HometoGo - Adelaide](https://www.hometogo.com.au/adelaide/)
- Description: HometoGo allows travelers to search and compare vacation rentals in Adelaide from various booking platforms, making it easy to find the perfect accommodation for your stay based on location, price, and amenities.

These vacation rental platforms offer a wide range of accommodations in Adelaide, allowing travelers to find the perfect home base for their stay in the city. Guests can browse listings, read reviews, and book directly through the websites for a seamless booking experience.

5. Dining and Cuisine

Local Specialties:

Adelaide's culinary scene is as diverse as it is delicious, offering a tantalizing array of local specialties that showcase the city's multicultural heritage and vibrant food culture. From fresh seafood and farm-fresh produce to innovative fusion dishes and traditional Aboriginal cuisine, Adelaide's local specialties are sure to delight food lovers and adventurous eaters alike.

1. Fritz: A beloved South Australian icon, Fritz is a type of processed meat similar to Devon or bologna, often enjoyed as a sandwich filling or fried as a snack. Made from finely ground pork, beef, and seasonings, Fritz is a nostalgic comfort food that has been enjoyed by generations of South Australians.

2. Pie Floater: A quintessential Adelaide dish, the Pie Floater consists of a meat pie topped with a generous serving of pea soup. Originating from the city's early street food scene, the Pie Floater is a hearty and satisfying meal that can be found at various food stalls, cafes, and bakeries throughout Adelaide.

3. Barramundi: With its proximity to the coastline, Adelaide boasts an abundance of fresh seafood, including the iconic Barramundi. Known for its firm white flesh and delicate flavor, Barramundi is a popular choice on restaurant menus and is often served grilled, pan-seared, or baked with seasonal accompaniments.

4. Coopers Beer: Founded in Adelaide in 1862, Coopers Brewery is Australia's largest and oldest family-owned brewery, known for its range of handcrafted beers and ales. From the classic Pale Ale to the refreshing Sparkling Ale and Stout, Coopers Beer is a local favorite enjoyed by beer enthusiasts across the country.

5. Chilli Crab: Reflecting Adelaide's multicultural influences, Chilli Crab is a popular dish in the city's vibrant Asian dining scene. Featuring mud crab cooked in a spicy tomato-based sauce infused with garlic, ginger, and chili, Chilli Crab is a flavorful and indulgent seafood dish that is best enjoyed with crusty bread or steamed rice.

6. Kangaroo: For a taste of Australia's native cuisine, adventurous diners can try Kangaroo meat, which is lean, flavorful, and rich in protein. Kangaroo steaks, burgers, and sausages can be found on the menus of many Adelaide restaurants, offering a unique and sustainable dining experience.

7. Aboriginal Bush Foods: Adelaide's culinary landscape also includes a growing appreciation for Indigenous Australian ingredients and traditional bush foods. From native herbs and spices to game meats and fruits, Aboriginal cuisine offers a unique opportunity to explore the flavors and culinary traditions of Australia's First Nations people.

8. Haigh's Chocolates: A South Australian institution since 1915, Haigh's Chocolates is renowned for its premium handcrafted chocolates and confections. From creamy truffles and smooth milk chocolate to decadent dark chocolate bars and specialty treats, Haigh's Chocolates is a must-visit destination for chocolate lovers in Adelaide.

These local specialties represent just a taste of Adelaide's diverse and dynamic culinary scene, where flavors from around the world come together to create a delicious and unforgettable dining experience. Whether you're craving classic comfort foods, exotic flavors, or innovative culinary creations, Adelaide has something to satisfy every palate and craving.

Restaurants:

Adelaide boasts a vibrant dining scene with a diverse array of restaurants offering cuisines from around the world, as well as showcasing the best of South Australian produce and culinary talent. From fine dining establishments to casual eateries and hidden gems, here are some noteworthy restaurants in Adelaide:

1. Orana
   - Website: [Orana](https://restaurantorana.com/)
   - Description: Helmed by acclaimed chef Jock Zonfrillo, Orana is renowned for its innovative tasting menus that celebrate Indigenous Australian ingredients and culinary traditions. Located in the heart of Adelaide's CBD, Orana offers a unique and immersive dining experience that highlights the diversity and richness of Australian cuisine.

2. Penfolds Magill Estate Restaurant
   - Website: [Penfolds Magill Estate Restaurant](https://www.penfolds.com/en-au/magill-estate-restaurant)
   - Description: Nestled within the historic Magill Estate winery, Penfolds Magill Estate Restaurant offers a sophisticated dining experience showcasing contemporary Australian cuisine paired with world-class wines from the Penfolds portfolio. Set against a backdrop of vineyards and rolling hills, the restaurant provides an elegant setting for special occasions and celebrations.

3. Africola
   - Website: [Africola](https://www.africola.com.au/)
   - Description: Africola is a vibrant and eclectic eatery specializing in modern African cuisine with a twist. Led by chef Duncan Welgemoed, the restaurant serves up bold and flavorsome dishes inspired by the diverse culinary traditions of the African continent, accompanied by an extensive selection of cocktails, natural wines, and craft beers.

4. Press Food & Wine
   - Website: [Press Food & Wine](https://www.pressfoodandwine.com.au/)
   - Description: Located in Adelaide's bustling East End, Press Food & Wine is a contemporary bistro known for its seasonal menus, extensive wine list, and relaxed yet stylish ambiance. The restaurant offers a diverse range of dishes highlighting local and regional produce, with an emphasis on flavor and quality.

5. Botanic Gardens Restaurant
   - Website: [Botanic Gardens Restaurant](https://www.botanicgardensrestaurant.com.au/)
   - Description: Situated within the lush surroundings of the Adelaide Botanic Garden, Botanic Gardens Restaurant offers an elegant dining experience overlooking the garden's tranquil lawns and water features. The restaurant's menu showcases modern Australian cuisine with an emphasis on fresh, seasonal ingredients sourced from local producers.

6. Golden Boy
   - Website: [Golden Boy](https://www.golden-boy.com.au/)

- Description: Golden Boy is a stylish and contemporary Thai restaurant located in Adelaide's historic East End. Offering a modern twist on traditional Thai flavors, the restaurant's menu features a selection of small and large plates designed for sharing, along with an extensive cocktail list and eclectic wine selection.

7. Shobosho
   - Website: [Shobosho] (https://www.shobosho.com.au/)
   - Description: Shobosho is a Japanese-inspired grill and bar located in Adelaide's bustling Leigh Street precinct. Led by chef Adam Liston, the restaurant's menu showcases wood-fired cooking techniques and bold flavors, with a focus on locally sourced ingredients and seasonal produce.

8. Andre's Cucina & Polenta Bar
   - Website: [Andre's Cucina & Polenta Bar] (https://andrescucina.com.au/)
   - Description: Andre's Cucina & Polenta Bar is a cozy and charming Italian eatery located in Adelaide's CBD. Specializing in rustic Italian fare with a focus on house-made pastas and polenta dishes, the restaurant offers a warm and welcoming atmosphere perfect for casual dining and gatherings with friends and family.

These restaurants represent just a selection of Adelaide's diverse dining scene, offering a range of culinary experiences to suit every taste and occasion. Reservations are recommended for many of these establishments, especially during peak dining hours and on weekends.

Cafes:

Adelaide is dotted with charming cafes serving up delicious coffee, freshly baked pastries, and hearty brunch fare. Whether you're in search of a cozy spot to enjoy a leisurely breakfast, a stylish cafe for a mid-morning pick-me-up, or a relaxed setting for catching up with friends over lunch, Adelaide's cafe scene has something for everyone. Here are some noteworthy cafes to check out:

1. Coffee Branch
   - Description: Tucked away in Adelaide's East End, Coffee Branch is a popular cafe known for its specialty coffee, friendly service, and inviting atmosphere. The cafe serves up a range of artisanal coffee blends alongside a selection of sweet and savory treats, making it a favorite spot for locals and visitors alike.
   - Website: [Coffee Branch] (https://coffeebranch.com.au/)

2. Exchange Specialty Coffee
   - Description: Located in the historic Adelaide Arcade, Exchange Specialty Coffee is a specialty coffee roastery and cafe known for its meticulously crafted brews and stylish interior. The cafe offers a rotating selection of single-origin coffees and espresso blends, as well as a menu of gourmet toasties, sandwiches, and pastries.
   - Website: [Exchange Specialty Coffee] (https://www.exchangecoffee.com.au/)

3. Peter Rabbit
   - Description: Nestled in a charming courtyard in Adelaide's CBD, Peter Rabbit is a whimsical cafe and garden bar offering a relaxed and family-friendly atmosphere. The cafe's menu features a range of fresh and seasonal dishes made with locally sourced ingredients, along with an array of artisanal beverages and homemade cakes.

- Website: [Peter Rabbit] (https://peterrabbit.com.au/)

4. Fine and Fettle
   - Description: Fine and Fettle is a stylish cafe located in the leafy suburb of Stepney, known for its modern Australian cuisine and specialty coffee. The cafe's menu features a range of healthy and flavorful dishes, including breakfast bowls, gourmet sandwiches, and vibrant salads, all served in a chic and contemporary setting.
   - Website: [Fine and Fettle] (https://fineandfettle.com.au/)

5. Eggless Dessert Cafe
   - Description: Catering to those with a sweet tooth, Eggless Dessert Cafe is a popular spot for indulging in decadent desserts and treats. Specializing in egg-free and vegan desserts, the cafe offers a tempting array of cakes, pastries, and desserts, as well as a selection of hot and cold beverages.
   - Website: [Eggless Dessert Cafe] (https://www.egglesscafe.com.au/)

6. The Loose Caboose
   - Description: Housed in a converted railway carriage in the suburb of Bowden, The Loose Caboose is a quirky cafe known for its creative brunch dishes and relaxed vibe. The cafe's menu features a range of breakfast classics with a twist, as well as gourmet burgers, salads, and house-made cakes and pastries.
   - Website: [The Loose Caboose] (https://www.theloosecaboose.com.au/)

7. Hey Jupiter
   - Description: Inspired by the cafes of Paris, Hey Jupiter is a cozy French bistro and cafe located in Adelaide's East

End. The cafe's menu features classic French dishes alongside Australian favorites, with an emphasis on locally sourced ingredients and artisanal produce. Guests can enjoy breakfast, lunch, or a leisurely coffee in the charming indoor space or outdoor courtyard.
   - Website: [Hey Jupiter] (https://www.heyjupiter.com.au/)

8. The Flinders Street Project
   - Description: Situated in the bustling suburb of Kent Town, The Flinders Street Project is a contemporary cafe known for its seasonal menus, specialty coffee, and creative culinary offerings. The cafe's menu features a range of breakfast and lunch options, with an emphasis on fresh, locally sourced ingredients and innovative flavor combinations.
   - Website: [The Flinders Street Project] (https://www.flindersstreetproject.com.au/)

These cafes offer a delightful mix of ambiance, quality food, and excellent coffee, making them ideal spots to relax and indulge in Adelaide's thriving cafe culture. Whether you're craving a hearty breakfast, a leisurely brunch, or a sweet treat, you're sure to find something to satisfy your cravings at one of these local favorites.

Food Markets:

Exploring Adelaide's food markets is a feast for the senses, offering an abundance of fresh produce, gourmet delights, and local specialties. From bustling farmers' markets to vibrant multicultural markets, these culinary destinations provide an opportunity to discover the flavors and ingredients that make Adelaide's food scene so unique. Here are some must-visit food markets in Adelaide:

1. Adelaide Central Market
   - Description: Established in 1869, the Adelaide Central Market is a beloved institution and one of the largest undercover fresh produce markets in the Southern Hemisphere. With over 80 stalls showcasing a diverse range of fruits, vegetables, meats, seafood, cheeses, baked goods, and gourmet delights, the market is a paradise for food lovers and culinary enthusiasts. Visitors can explore the market's bustling aisles, sample artisanal products, and enjoy delicious meals from the market's cafes and eateries.
   - Website: [Adelaide Central Market] (https://adelaidecentralmarket.com.au/)

2. Barossa Farmers Market
   - Description: Located in the heart of South Australia's renowned Barossa Valley wine region, the Barossa Farmers Market is a vibrant community market showcasing the best of local produce and artisanal goods. Held every Saturday morning, the market features a wide selection of seasonal fruits and vegetables, smallgoods, cheeses, breads, pastries, and gourmet treats, all sourced directly from local farmers, producers, and artisans.
   - Website: [Barossa Farmers Market] (https://www.barossafarmersmarket.com/)

3. Adelaide Showground Farmers' Market
   - Description: Held every Sunday at the Adelaide Showground, the Adelaide Showground Farmers' Market is a bustling market featuring a wide range of fresh produce, gourmet foods, and handmade products from local farmers, producers, and artisans. Visitors can browse the stalls, chat with the vendors, and enjoy live music and entertainment while sampling delicious foods and stocking up on pantry essentials.

- Website: [Adelaide Showground Farmers' Market] (https://adelaidefarmersmarket.com.au/)

4. Gilles Street Market
   - Description: A treasure trove of vintage fashion, handmade crafts, and gourmet treats, the Gilles Street Market is a popular Sunday market held in Adelaide's trendy West End. In addition to fashion and design stalls, the market also features a selection of food trucks and vendors offering a diverse range of street food, artisanal snacks, and sweet treats to enjoy while browsing the stalls.
   - Website: [Gilles Street Market] (https://gillesstreetmarket.com.au/)

5. Flinders Street Market
   - Description: Nestled in the historic suburb of Bowden, the Flinders Street Market is a vibrant community market showcasing the work of local artists, designers, and makers. In addition to arts and crafts stalls, the market also features a selection of food vendors offering a variety of gourmet delights, including baked goods, chocolates, preserves, and more.
   - Website: [Flinders Street Market] (https://www.flindersstreetmarket.com.au/)

6. Plant 4 Bowden
   - Description: Located in the redeveloped Bowden precinct, Plant 4 Bowden is a bustling marketplace featuring a diverse range of food vendors, artisanal producers, and specialty retailers. The market offers everything from fresh produce and gourmet groceries to street food, international cuisines, and specialty coffee, providing a vibrant and eclectic dining experience for visitors to enjoy.

- Website: [Plant 4 Bowden] (https://plant4bowden.com.au/)

7. Willunga Farmers Market
- Description: Located in the picturesque McLaren Vale wine region, the Willunga Farmers Market is a thriving community market showcasing the best of local produce and artisanal products from the Fleurieu Peninsula. Held every Saturday morning, the market offers a wide selection of seasonal fruits and vegetables, organic meats, cheeses, breads, and gourmet treats, all sourced directly from local growers and producers.
- Website: [Willunga Farmers Market] (https://willungafarmersmarket.com.au/)

8. Semaphore Street Fair
- Description: The Semaphore Street Fair is an annual event held in the seaside suburb of Semaphore, featuring a lively market atmosphere with stalls selling a variety of goods, including crafts, clothing, homewares, and gourmet foods. Visitors can explore the bustling streets, enjoy live music and entertainment, and sample delicious foods from local vendors while soaking up the vibrant atmosphere of this popular community event.
- Website: [Semaphore Street Fair] (https://semaphorestreetfair.com.au/)

These food markets offer a delightful opportunity to experience the vibrant flavors, aromas, and atmosphere of Adelaide's culinary scene, while supporting local producers and artisans. Whether you're shopping for fresh ingredients, sampling gourmet treats, or simply enjoying the lively ambiance, a visit to one of these markets is sure to be a memorable experience.

6. Attractions in Adelaide

Adelaide Botanic Garden:

The Adelaide Botanic Garden is an oasis of tranquility and natural beauty located in the heart of the city. Spanning 51 hectares, the garden features a diverse collection of plants from around the world, including native Australian flora, exotic specimens, and themed gardens. Visitors can explore winding pathways, picturesque ponds, and historic buildings, including the iconic Palm House and Bicentennial Conservatory. The garden also hosts events, guided tours, and educational programs for all ages.
- Website: [Adelaide Botanic Garden] (https://www.botanicgardens.sa.gov.au/visit/adelaide-botanic-garden)

Adelaide Zoo:

Founded in 1883, the Adelaide Zoo is home to a fascinating array of animals from Australia and around the globe. Spread across 8 hectares, the zoo features spacious enclosures and naturalistic habitats where visitors can observe rare and endangered species up close. Highlights include the Giant Panda Forest, where visitors can see Adelaide's resident giant pandas, as well as exhibits showcasing native wildlife, primates, big cats, and more. The zoo also offers behind-the-scenes experiences, animal encounters, and educational programs.
- Website: [Adelaide Zoo] (https://www.adelaidezoo.com.au/)

Adelaide Central Market:

The Adelaide Central Market is a bustling hub of culinary delights and cultural diversity, offering a sensory feast for visitors. Established in 1869, the market is one of the largest undercover fresh produce markets in the Southern Hemisphere, with over 80 stalls showcasing a wide range of fresh fruits, vegetables, meats, seafood, cheeses, baked goods, and gourmet treats. Visitors can explore the market's vibrant aisles, sample artisanal products, and enjoy delicious meals from the market's cafes and eateries.
- Website: [Adelaide Central Market] (https://adelaidecentralmarket.com.au/)

Adelaide Oval:

Renowned as one of Australia's most iconic sporting venues, the Adelaide Oval is a must-visit destination for sports fans and architecture enthusiasts alike. Located on the banks of the River Torrens, the oval has a rich history dating back to 1871 and has hosted countless cricket matches, football games, concerts, and events over the years. Visitors can take guided tours of the stadium to learn about its heritage and explore behind the scenes, including the player facilities, media center, and heritage-listed scoreboard.
- Website: [Adelaide Oval] (https://www.adelaideoval.com.au/)

Art Gallery of South Australia:

The Art Gallery of South Australia is a premier cultural institution showcasing an extensive collection of Australian, Indigenous, and international art spanning centuries. Located in the heart of Adelaide's cultural precinct, the gallery's permanent collection includes paintings, sculptures, decorative arts, and works on paper by renowned artists such as Tom Roberts, Sidney Nolan, and Emily Kame Kngwarreye. The gallery also hosts temporary exhibitions, public programs, and educational activities for visitors of all ages.

- Website: [Art Gallery of South Australia](https://www.agsa.sa.gov.au/)

South Australian Museum:
Founded in 1856, the South Australian Museum is a leading natural history and cultural institution dedicated to preserving and sharing the heritage of South Australia and the world. The museum's extensive collections include fossils, minerals, ethnographic artifacts, and indigenous cultural objects, as well as exhibits showcasing the natural history and biodiversity of the region. Highlights include the Ancient Egypt gallery, the Australian Aboriginal Cultures gallery, and the Megafauna gallery, which features giant prehistoric animals that once roamed the continent.

- Website: [South Australian Museum](https://www.samuseum.sa.gov.au/)

Adelaide Hills:

The Adelaide Hills region is a picturesque destination located just a short drive from the city center, offering stunning natural scenery, charming towns, and a wealth of outdoor activities. Visitors can explore quaint villages, sample local produce at roadside stalls and farm gates, and embark on scenic drives through rolling hills and lush vineyards. Popular attractions in the Adelaide Hills include Mount Lofty Summit, Cleland Wildlife Park, Hahndorf, and the Mount Lofty Botanic Garden.

- Website: [Adelaide Hills Tourism] (https://www.adelaidehills.org.au/)

Glenelg Beach:
Glenelg Beach is Adelaide's premier seaside destination, renowned for its golden sands, pristine waters, and vibrant atmosphere. Located just 20 minutes from the city center, Glenelg offers a wide range of activities for visitors to enjoy, including swimming, surfing, paddleboarding, and beach volleyball. The lively Jetty Road precinct is lined with cafes, restaurants, boutique shops, and attractions such as the Glenelg Tram and the Beachouse amusement park.
- Website: [Glenelg Beach] (https://www.glenelgbeach.com/)

Hahndorf (German village):
Hahndorf is Australia's oldest surviving German settlement and a charming destination steeped in history, culture, and old-world charm. Located in the Adelaide Hills, Hahndorf is known for its picturesque main street lined with quaint shops, galleries, cafes, and traditional German pubs serving hearty meals and locally brewed beers. Visitors can explore historic buildings, admire traditional Bavarian architecture, and sample delicious German cuisine and artisanal products.
- Website: [Hahndorf Tourism] (https://www.hahndorfsa.org.au/)

Barossa Valley (Wine region):
The Barossa Valley is one of Australia's most renowned wine regions, celebrated for its world-class wines, picturesque vineyards, and rich culinary heritage. Located just an hour's drive north of Adelaide, the Barossa is home to over 150 wineries, ranging from boutique family-owned estates to iconic wine labels known around the world. Visitors can enjoy wine tastings and cellar door experiences, dine at award-winning restaurants, and

explore the region's historic towns, artisanal food producers, and scenic landscapes.
- Website: [Barossa - Be Consumed] (https://www.barossa.com/)

These attractions offer a diverse range of experiences, from coastal escapes and cultural heritage to gourmet delights and outdoor adventures, making them must-visit destinations for travelers exploring Adelaide and its surrounds.

7. Cultural Experiences

Festivals and Events:

Adelaide is renowned for its vibrant calendar of festivals and events, showcasing the city's rich cultural diversity, artistic talent, and spirit of celebration. From world-class arts festivals to food and wine events, music concerts, and multicultural celebrations, there's always something exciting happening in Adelaide throughout the year. Here are some of the city's standout festivals and events:

1. Adelaide Festival:
   - Description: The Adelaide Festival is one of Australia's premier arts festivals, presenting a diverse program of theater, dance, music, visual arts, and literature from around the world. Held annually in March, the festival attracts leading artists, performers, and creatives to Adelaide for a month-long celebration of culture and creativity.
   - Website: [Adelaide Festival] (https://www.adelaidefestival.com.au/)

2. Adelaide Fringe:
   - Description: The Adelaide Fringe is the largest arts festival in the Southern Hemisphere and one of the most vibrant and diverse fringe festivals in the world. Held annually from February to March, the festival features thousands of performances across various art forms, including comedy, cabaret, circus, theater, music, and visual arts, transforming Adelaide into a lively hub of creativity and entertainment.
   - Website: [Adelaide Fringe] (https://adelaidefringe.com.au/)

3. Tasting Australia:

- Description: Tasting Australia is Australia's premier food and wine festival, celebrating the country's diverse culinary landscape and showcasing the best of South Australian produce, wines, and culinary talent. Held biennially in Adelaide, the festival features a program of food and wine events, cooking demonstrations, tastings, masterclasses, and long-table lunches, offering visitors the opportunity to indulge in a gastronomic feast.
- Website: [Tasting Australia] (https://tastingaustralia.com.au/)

4. Santos Tour Down Under:

- Description: The Santos Tour Down Under is Australia's premier cycling race and the first event on the UCI WorldTour calendar. Held annually in January, the race attracts top cyclists from around the world to compete in a series of stages across South Australia, with Adelaide serving as the race hub. In addition to the professional race, the event also features community rides, cycling tours, and family-friendly activities.
- Website: [Santos Tour Down Under] (https://tourdownunder.com.au/)

5. WOMADelaide:

- Description: WOMADelaide is an annual world music and dance festival held in Adelaide's Botanic Park, featuring a diverse lineup of artists from around the globe. Celebrating cultural diversity, creativity, and artistic expression, the festival offers a vibrant program of music, performances, workshops, talks, and visual arts, creating a unique and immersive cultural experience for audiences of all ages.
- Website: [WOMADelaide] (https://www.womadelaide.com.au/)

6. OzAsia Festival:
   - Description: The OzAsia Festival is Australia's leading contemporary arts festival focusing on Asia, presenting a diverse program of theater, dance, music, film, visual arts, and literature from across the Asia-Pacific region. Held annually in Adelaide, the festival highlights the cultural connections between Australia and Asia, fostering cross-cultural exchange and dialogue through artistic collaboration and innovation.
   - Website: [OzAsia Festival] (https://www.ozasiafestival.com.au/)

These festivals and events offer unique opportunities to immerse yourself in Adelaide's vibrant cultural scene, discover new artistic perspectives, and celebrate the city's diverse cultural heritage and creative spirit. Whether you're a fan of the performing arts, culinary delights, or outdoor spectacles, there's something for everyone to enjoy at Adelaide's festivals and events throughout the year.

Theatres and Performing Arts:

Adelaide is a hub for theatres and performing arts venues, offering a diverse range of productions, from world-class theater performances and musicals to dance, opera, and comedy shows. Whether you're a fan of classic dramas, contemporary dance, or cutting-edge experimental theater, Adelaide's vibrant arts scene has something to offer for every taste and preference. Here are some of the city's prominent theatres and performing arts venues:

1. Adelaide Festival Centre:
   - Description: The Adelaide Festival Centre is the premier performing arts venue in South Australia, housing multiple theaters and performance spaces, including the iconic

Festival Theatre, Dunstan Playhouse, Space Theatre, and Her Majesty's Theatre. The center hosts a year-round program of theater productions, musicals, dance performances, concerts, and festivals, showcasing local, national, and international talent.

   - Website: [Adelaide Festival Centre] (https://www.adelaidefestivalcentre.com.au/)

2. Her Majesty's Theatre:

   - Description: Originally opened in 1913, Her Majesty's Theatre is one of Adelaide's oldest and most iconic theaters, known for its stunning Edwardian architecture and rich heritage. Following an extensive renovation and restoration, the theater has been transformed into a state-of-the-art venue equipped with modern facilities while retaining its historic charm. Her Majesty's Theatre hosts a variety of performances, including musicals, dramas, concerts, and comedy shows.

   - Website: [Her Majesty's Theatre] (https://www.adelaidefestivalcentre.com.au/venues/her-majestys-theatre/)

3. State Theatre Company South Australia:

   - Description: The State Theatre Company South Australia is the state's flagship professional theater company, dedicated to producing high-quality theatrical productions that inspire, challenge, and entertain audiences. The company performs a diverse repertoire of classic and contemporary works, including Australian premieres, new commissions, and reimagined interpretations of classic texts, at venues across Adelaide.

   - Website: [State Theatre Company South Australia] (https://statetheatrecompany.com.au/)

4. Adelaide Repertory Theatre:

- Description: The Adelaide Repertory Theatre is one of Adelaide's oldest and most respected community theater companies, known for its commitment to producing quality theatrical productions by local talent. Established in 1908, the company presents a varied program of plays, musicals, and cabaret shows at its intimate theater space in the suburb of Kensington.
   - Website: [Adelaide Repertory Theatre] (https://adelaiderep.com/)

5. The Space Theatre:
   - Description: The Space Theatre is a contemporary performance venue located within the Adelaide Festival Centre complex, dedicated to presenting innovative and experimental works by local, national, and international artists. The theater's flexible seating arrangement and state-of-the-art technical facilities make it an ideal space for immersive theater experiences, contemporary dance performances, and experimental productions.
   - Website: [The Space Theatre] (https://www.adelaidefestivalcentre.com.au/venues/the-space-theatre/)

6. Umbrella Festival:
   - Description: The Umbrella Festival is an annual open-access arts festival celebrating South Australia's vibrant independent arts scene, with a focus on music, theater, cabaret, comedy, and spoken word performances. Held across multiple venues in Adelaide, the festival showcases emerging and established artists, providing opportunities for creative expression, collaboration, and experimentation.
   - Website: [Umbrella Festival] (https://www.umbrellafestival.com.au/)

These theaters and performing arts venues are at the heart of Adelaide's cultural landscape, providing platforms for artistic expression, creativity, and entertainment. Whether you're a theater enthusiast, dance aficionado, or music lover, you'll find a wealth of captivating performances to enjoy at Adelaide's theaters and performing arts venues throughout the year.

Museums and Galleries:

Adelaide boasts a rich cultural heritage and a thriving arts scene, with a diverse range of museums and galleries showcasing everything from ancient artifacts and indigenous art to contemporary masterpieces and interactive exhibits. Whether you're interested in history, art, science, or culture, Adelaide's museums and galleries offer immersive experiences that inspire, educate, and entertain. Here are some of the city's notable museums and galleries:

1. Art Gallery of South Australia:
   - Description: The Art Gallery of South Australia is home to one of the country's most extensive art collections, featuring Australian, Indigenous, and international artworks spanning centuries. The gallery's permanent collection includes paintings, sculptures, decorative arts, and works on paper by renowned artists such as Sidney Nolan, Hans Heysen, and Emily Kame Kngwarreye. The gallery also hosts temporary exhibitions, public programs, and educational activities.
   - Website: [Art Gallery of South Australia] (https://www.agsa.sa.gov.au/)

2. South Australian Museum:

- Description: The South Australian Museum is a leading natural history and cultural institution, dedicated to preserving and sharing the heritage of South Australia and the world. The museum's extensive collections include fossils, minerals, ethnographic artifacts, and indigenous cultural objects, as well as exhibits showcasing the natural history and biodiversity of the region. Highlights include the Ancient Egypt gallery, the Australian Aboriginal Cultures gallery, and the Megafauna gallery.
   - Website: [South Australian Museum](https://www.samuseum.sa.gov.au/)

3. **Migration Museum**:
   - Description: The Migration Museum explores the diverse stories and experiences of migrants who have made South Australia their home, celebrating the cultural diversity and contributions of migrant communities to the state. The museum's exhibitions explore themes such as migration journeys, cultural identity, settlement experiences, and the impact of immigration on society, through a range of artifacts, photographs, oral histories, and interactive displays.
   - Website: [Migration Museum](https://migration.history.sa.gov.au/)

4. **JamFactory:**
   - Description: JamFactory is a contemporary art and design studio located in the heart of Adelaide's West End, dedicated to promoting and supporting Australian artists and designers working in glass, ceramics, metal, and jewelry. The studio offers gallery spaces showcasing exhibitions of contemporary craft and design, as well as a retail shop selling unique handmade objects and artworks.
   - Website: [JamFactory](https://www.jamfactory.com.au/)

5. National Railway Museum:
- Description: The National Railway Museum is Australia's largest railway museum, housing an extensive collection of locomotives, carriages, and railway memorabilia dating back to the early days of rail transport. Located in the historic port precinct of Port Adelaide, the museum offers visitors the opportunity to explore restored steam engines, diesel locomotives, and passenger carriages, as well as interactive exhibits, model railways, and guided tours.
- Website: [National Railway Museum] (https://nrm.org.au/)

6. Anne & Gordon Samstag Museum of Art:
- Description: The Anne & Gordon Samstag Museum of Art is a contemporary art museum located at the University of South Australia's City West campus, dedicated to showcasing the work of emerging and established contemporary artists from Australia and around the world. The museum's exhibitions feature a diverse range of mediums and styles, including painting, sculpture, photography, video, and installation art.
- Website: [Anne & Gordon Samstag Museum of Art] (https://www.unisa.edu.au/samstagmuseum/)

These museums and galleries offer engaging and thought-provoking experiences for visitors of all ages, providing opportunities to explore art, culture, history, and science in dynamic and interactive ways. Whether you're interested in ancient artifacts, contemporary art, or local heritage, you'll find a wealth of fascinating exhibits to discover at Adelaide's museums and galleries.

Aboriginal Culture Experiences:

Adelaide and its surrounding regions offer opportunities for visitors to engage with and learn about the rich and diverse cultures of Australia's Aboriginal peoples. From immersive cultural tours and educational experiences to art galleries and heritage sites, there are numerous ways to explore and appreciate Aboriginal culture in and around Adelaide. Here are some recommended Aboriginal culture experiences:

1. **Tandanya National Aboriginal Cultural Institute**:
    - Description: Tandanya is Australia's oldest Aboriginal-owned and operated cultural center, dedicated to showcasing and celebrating Aboriginal and Torres Strait Islander arts, culture, and heritage. Located in Adelaide's East End, Tandanya offers visitors the opportunity to explore contemporary and traditional Indigenous artworks, performances, exhibitions, and cultural events. The center also hosts workshops, talks, and educational programs that provide insights into Aboriginal culture and history.
    - Website: [Tandanya National Aboriginal Cultural Institute](https://tandanya.com.au/)

2. **Cultural Tours and Experiences**:
    - Description: Several tour operators in and around Adelaide offer guided cultural tours and experiences that provide insights into Aboriginal culture, traditions, and connections to the land. These tours may include visits to significant cultural sites, bushwalks, storytelling sessions, and opportunities to learn about traditional hunting, gathering, and bush tucker. Aboriginal guides share their knowledge, stories, and perspectives, offering visitors a deeper understanding of Aboriginal culture and heritage.
    - Website: Search for local tour operators offering Aboriginal cultural experiences.

3. Adelaide Park Lands Art and Heritage Trail:
   - Description: The Adelaide Park Lands Art and Heritage Trail is a self-guided walking trail that showcases artworks and cultural sites of significance within Adelaide's parklands. Along the trail, visitors can discover Aboriginal heritage markers, sculptures, and interpretive signs that highlight the cultural and historical significance of the land to the Kaurna people, the traditional custodians of the Adelaide Plains. The trail provides opportunities to learn about Kaurna culture, language, and connection to country.
   - Website: [Adelaide Park Lands Art and Heritage Trail] (https://www.cityofadelaide.com.au/explore-the-city/city-map-guides/adelaide-park-lands/art-and-heritage-trail/)

4. Aboriginal Art Galleries:
   - Description: Adelaide is home to several galleries and art spaces that specialize in showcasing Aboriginal art and supporting Indigenous artists. These galleries offer a diverse range of artworks, including paintings, sculptures, textiles, and ceramics, created by both established and emerging Aboriginal artists from across Australia. Visitors can explore exhibitions, meet artists, and purchase authentic Aboriginal artworks, supporting Indigenous communities and cultural preservation.
   - Website: Search for Aboriginal art galleries in Adelaide.

5. Cultural Festivals and Events:
   - Description: Adelaide hosts various festivals and events throughout the year that celebrate Aboriginal culture, including NAIDOC Week, Reconciliation Week, and Indigenous cultural festivals. These events feature performances, music, dance, art exhibitions, workshops, and community celebrations, providing opportunities for

people of all backgrounds to engage with and learn about Aboriginal culture, history, and contributions to Australian society.

- Website: Look for announcements and schedules of cultural festivals and events in Adelaide.

These Aboriginal culture experiences offer meaningful opportunities for visitors to engage with and learn about the rich cultural heritage and traditions of Australia's First Nations peoples, fostering understanding, respect, and appreciation for Aboriginal culture and perspectives.

8. Outdoor Activities

Hiking and Bushwalking:

Adelaide and its surrounding regions are blessed with stunning natural landscapes, offering countless opportunities for hiking and bushwalking enthusiasts to explore scenic trails, rugged coastlines, and lush wilderness areas. Whether you're a seasoned hiker seeking challenging terrain or a leisurely walker looking for a peaceful stroll, there are trails suited to all levels of experience and fitness. Here are some recommended hiking and bushwalking destinations near Adelaide:

1. Cleland Conservation Park:
   - Description: Located in the Adelaide Hills, Cleland Conservation Park is a picturesque natural reserve renowned for its diverse flora and fauna, including native wildlife such as kangaroos, koalas, and emus. The park offers a network of walking trails ranging from easy strolls to more challenging hikes, providing opportunities to explore scenic vistas, waterfalls, and tranquil forested areas. Popular trails include the Waterfall Gully to Mount Lofty Summit trail, the Waterfall Hike, and the Wood Duck Walk.
   - Website: [Cleland Conservation Park] (https://www.environment.sa.gov.au/parks/find-a-park/Browse_by_region/Adelaide_Hills/cleland-conservation-park)

2. Belair National Park:
   - Description: Belair National Park is South Australia's oldest national park and a popular destination for outdoor enthusiasts, offering a range of walking trails amid scenic bushland and native woodlands. The park features trails

suitable for all ages and fitness levels, including the popular Waterfall Hike to the picturesque First Falls, the Valley Loop Trail through fern gullies and native bird habitats, and the Echo Tunnel and Adventure Loop trails for more adventurous hikers.
   - Website: [Belair National Park] (https://www.environment.sa.gov.au/parks/find-a-park/Browse_by_region/Adelaide_Hills/belair-national-park)

3. Onkaparinga River National Park:
   - Description: Situated south of Adelaide, Onkaparinga River National Park encompasses rugged gorge landscapes, tranquil wetlands, and scenic coastal cliffs along the Onkaparinga River and Gulf St Vincent. The park offers a variety of walking trails that wind through native bushland, providing opportunities to spot native wildlife and enjoy panoramic views of the surrounding countryside and coastline. Highlights include the Punchbowl Lookout Trail, the Sundews Ridge Trail, and the Gorge Track.
   - Website: [Onkaparinga River National Park] (https://www.parks.sa.gov.au/find-a-park/Browse_by_region/Fleurieu_Peninsula/onkaparinga-river-national-park)

4. Mount Lofty Botanic Garden:
   - Description: Nestled within the Adelaide Hills, Mount Lofty Botanic Garden is a tranquil oasis showcasing a diverse collection of native and exotic plants from around the world. The garden offers a network of walking trails that meander through themed sections, including the Australian Native Garden, the Rhododendron Gully, and the Fern Gully, providing opportunities to explore picturesque landscapes, serene water features, and seasonal blooms.
   - Website: [Mount Lofty Botanic Garden]

(https://www.botanicgardens.sa.gov.au/visit/mount-lofty-botanic-garden)

5. Morialta Conservation Park:
   - Description: Morialta Conservation Park is a scenic natural reserve located in the Adelaide foothills, renowned for its rugged gorges, towering cliffs, and cascading waterfalls. The park offers a range of walking trails catering to all fitness levels, from short easy walks to more challenging hikes. Highlights include the First Falls Valley Walk, the Second Falls and Giants Cave Hike, and the scenic climb to Morialta Falls.
   - Website: [Morialta Conservation Park] (https://www.environment.sa.gov.au/parks/find-a-park/Browse_by_region/Adelaide_Hills/morialta-conservation-park)

These hiking and bushwalking destinations near Adelaide offer opportunities to connect with nature, unwind in serene surroundings, and discover the beauty of South Australia's diverse landscapes. Whether you're seeking panoramic viewpoints, lush forest trails, or coastal vistas, you'll find a multitude of outdoor adventures to enjoy in and around Adelaide.

Cycling Trails:

Adelaide and its surrounding regions offer a network of scenic cycling trails that cater to cyclists of all skill levels, from leisurely riders to experienced enthusiasts. Whether you prefer smooth bike paths along riverbanks and coastlines or rugged mountain trails through bushland and national parks, there's a cycling route to suit every preference. Here are some recommended cycling trails near Adelaide:

1. River Torrens Linear Park Trail:
   - Description: The River Torrens Linear Park Trail follows the tranquil banks of the River Torrens, offering a scenic cycling route through Adelaide's picturesque parklands and urban landscapes. The trail stretches from the Adelaide Hills to the coast, passing through green parklands, lakes, and wetlands, with plenty of opportunities for picnics, birdwatching, and sightseeing along the way. Highlights include the Adelaide Botanic Garden, Adelaide Zoo, and Linear Park Wetlands.
   - Website: [River Torrens Linear Park Trail] (https://www.cycleinstead.com.au/rides/river-torrens-linear-park-trail)

2. Coast to Vines Rail Trail:
   - Description: The Coast to Vines Rail Trail is a scenic cycling route that follows the former railway line from Marino Rocks to Willunga, passing through vineyards, farmland, and coastal landscapes in the McLaren Vale wine region. The trail offers a mix of sealed and gravel paths, providing opportunities to explore charming towns, cellar doors, and scenic viewpoints along the way. Highlights include the Onkaparinga River Estuary, McLaren Vale township, and Willunga Hill.
   - Website: [Coast to Vines Rail Trail] (https://www.cycleinstead.com.au/rides/coast-to-vines-rail-trail)

3. Mike Turtur Bikeway (Coast Park Path):
   - Description: The Mike Turtur Bikeway, also known as the Coast Park Path, is a popular coastal cycling route that stretches along Adelaide's metropolitan coastline, offering panoramic views of sandy beaches, rocky headlands, and the sparkling waters of Gulf St Vincent. The bikeway connects the suburbs of Henley Beach, Glenelg, and

Brighton, providing a scenic and flat route suitable for cyclists of all ages and abilities.
   - Website: [Mike Turtur Bikeway] (https://www.cycleinstead.com.au/rides/mike-turtur-bikeway)

4. Sturt River Linear Park Trail:
   - Description: The Sturt River Linear Park Trail follows the meandering course of the Sturt River, offering a peaceful and scenic cycling route through Adelaide's southern suburbs and greenbelt reserves. The trail passes through tranquil bushland, wetlands, and recreational areas, providing opportunities to spot native wildlife and enjoy the serenity of nature close to the city. Highlights include the Warriparinga Wetlands, Oaklands Wetland and Reserve, and Marion Coastal Walking Trail.
   - Website: [Sturt River Linear Park Trail] (https://www.cycleinstead.com.au/rides/sturt-river-linear-park-trail)

5. Lofty Ranges Trails Network:
   - Description: The Lofty Ranges Trails Network encompasses a network of mountain biking trails in the Adelaide Hills and Mount Lofty Ranges, offering a variety of terrain and difficulty levels for off-road cycling enthusiasts. The network features purpose-built singletrack trails, fire tracks, and forest roads, winding through native bushland, pine forests, and conservation parks. Trails cater to beginners through to experienced riders, with options for short loops, long-distance rides, and technical challenges.
   - Website: [Lofty Ranges Trails Network] (https://www.samtb.org.au/)

These cycling trails near Adelaide provide opportunities to explore the region's natural beauty, cultural heritage, and scenic landscapes on two wheels, offering enjoyable and active outdoor experiences for cyclists of all abilities. Whether you're seeking coastal vistas, vineyard views, or bushland adventures, there's a cycling route to suit your preferences and interests in and around Adelaide.

Water Sports (Sailing, Kayaking, Surfing):

Adelaide's coastal location and proximity to pristine beaches and waterways make it an ideal destination for water sports enthusiasts seeking adventure and excitement on the water. Whether you're interested in sailing, kayaking, surfing, or other water-based activities, there are plenty of opportunities to enjoy the sun, surf, and sea in and around Adelaide. Here are some recommended water sports experiences near Adelaide:

1. Sailing:
   - Description: Adelaide's coastal waters offer excellent sailing opportunities for enthusiasts of all skill levels, with sheltered bays, open waters, and scenic coastal landscapes to explore. The Adelaide Sailing Club at West Beach and the Royal South Australian Yacht Squadron at Outer Harbor are popular sailing clubs that offer sailing lessons, yacht charters, and racing events for members and visitors. Whether you're a novice sailor or experienced skipper, there are sailing experiences to suit every interest and ability.
   - Website:
     - [Adelaide Sailing Club] (https://www.adelaidesailingclub.com.au/)
     - [Royal South Australian Yacht Squadron] (https://www.rsays.com.au/)

2. Kayaking:

- Description: Adelaide's rivers, estuaries, and coastal waters provide ideal conditions for kayaking and paddling adventures, offering opportunities to explore scenic waterways, wildlife habitats, and hidden coves. Popular kayaking destinations include the Onkaparinga River Estuary, Port Adelaide River, and Adelaide Dolphin Sanctuary at Garden Island. Guided kayak tours, equipment rentals, and lessons are available from various operators, allowing visitors to experience the beauty of Adelaide's waterways up close.
   - Website: Search for local kayak rental and tour operators.

3. Surfing:
   - Description: Adelaide's metropolitan coastline boasts some of South Australia's best surf breaks, attracting surfers from near and far to ride the waves year-round. Popular surfing beaches include Middleton, Moana, and Southport, which offer a variety of breaks suitable for surfers of all levels, from beginners to experienced riders. Surf schools and surf shops located along the coast provide equipment hire, surfing lessons, and surfboard repairs, catering to surfers looking to catch their first wave or improve their skills.
   - Website: Search for local surf schools and surf shops along Adelaide's coastline.

4. Stand-Up Paddleboarding (SUP):
   - Description: Stand-up paddleboarding (SUP) is a popular water sport that offers a fun and relaxing way to explore Adelaide's waterways and coastal scenery. Paddleboarding is suitable for all ages and fitness levels, providing a full-body workout while enjoying the tranquility of the water. Adelaide's calm bays, rivers, and estuaries are perfect for paddleboarding adventures, with

opportunities to spot marine life, paddle alongside dolphins, and admire scenic waterfront views.

  - Website: Search for local SUP rental and tour operators.

5. Windsurfing and Kitesurfing:

  - Description: Adelaide's windy coastal conditions make it an ideal destination for windsurfing and kitesurfing enthusiasts seeking high-adrenaline thrills on the water. Beaches such as Semaphore, West Beach, and Aldinga Beach are popular spots for windsurfing and kitesurfing, offering consistent wind conditions and ample space to ride the waves. Equipment rentals, lessons, and coaching clinics are available for beginners and experienced riders looking to master the art of windsurfing and kitesurfing.

  - Website: Search for local windsurfing and kitesurfing schools and equipment rental providers.

These water sports experiences near Adelaide provide opportunities for outdoor adventure, fitness, and enjoyment on the water, allowing visitors to immerse themselves in the region's natural beauty and coastal lifestyle. Whether you're sailing across azure waters, kayaking through tranquil estuaries, or catching waves at sunset, there's a water sport to suit every interest and ability in and around Adelaide.

Golf Courses:

Adelaide boasts a selection of picturesque golf courses set amid stunning natural landscapes, offering golfers of all levels the opportunity to enjoy a round of golf in beautiful surroundings. From championship courses designed by renowned architects to public courses suitable for casual play, there's a golfing experience to suit every preference and skill level. Here are some recommended golf courses near Adelaide:

1. Royal Adelaide Golf Club:
  - Description: Founded in 1892, the Royal Adelaide Golf Club is one of Australia's premier golfing destinations, renowned for its challenging championship layout, fast greens, and natural bushland setting. The course has hosted numerous national and international tournaments, attracting top players and enthusiasts from around the world. With its strategic bunkering, undulating fairways, and coastal breezes, Royal Adelaide offers a true test of golfing skill and strategy.
  - Website: [Royal Adelaide Golf Club] (https://www.royaladelaidegolf.com.au/)

2. Kooyonga Golf Club:
  - Description: Kooyonga Golf Club is a prestigious private golf club located in the western suburbs of Adelaide, featuring a championship course designed by legendary golf course architect C.B. Macdonald. Set amongst natural sand dunes and native vegetation, the course offers a challenging yet rewarding golfing experience, with strategic bunkering, water hazards, and undulating fairways. Kooyonga has hosted multiple national and international tournaments, showcasing its reputation as one of South Australia's finest golf courses.
  - Website: [Kooyonga Golf Club] (https://www.kooyongagolf.com.au/)

3. Glenelg Golf Club:
  - Description: Situated adjacent to the picturesque coastline of Glenelg, Glenelg Golf Club is a premier links-style golf course renowned for its stunning coastal views,

challenging layout, and fast-running fairways. Designed by renowned golf course architect Alister MacKenzie, the course offers a true links golfing experience, with sandy soils, natural dunes, and strategic bunkering providing a test of skill and shot-making ability. The club also offers excellent practice facilities, including a driving range, putting greens, and short game area.

   - Website: [Glenelg Golf Club] (https://www.glenelggolf.com/)

4. The Grange Golf Club:

   - Description: The Grange Golf Club is a prestigious private golf club located in the western suburbs of Adelaide, featuring two championship courses: the East Course and the West Course. Designed by renowned golf course architect Greg Norman, the East Course is a challenging layout with strategic bunkering, water hazards, and native vegetation, while the West Course offers a more forgiving and picturesque setting with wide fairways and scenic views. Both courses provide an enjoyable and memorable golfing experience for players of all abilities.

   - Website: [The Grange Golf Club] (https://www.grangegolf.com.au/)

5. Mount Osmond Golf Club:

   - Description: Nestled in the Adelaide Hills, Mount Osmond Golf Club offers a unique golfing experience amidst native bushland and panoramic views of the city and coastline below. The course features undulating fairways, challenging greens, and tight tree-lined fairways, providing golfers with a scenic and challenging test of skill and accuracy. With its natural beauty and serene setting, Mount Osmond is a popular choice for golfers seeking a tranquil escape from the hustle and bustle of city life.

   - Website: [Mount Osmond Golf Club] (https://www.mogc.com.au/)

These golf courses near Adelaide offer golfers the opportunity to experience the natural beauty and challenging layouts that South Australia has to offer, providing memorable and rewarding golfing experiences for players of all levels. Whether you're a seasoned pro or a casual player, you'll find a course to suit your preferences and skill level in and around Adelaide.

Wildlife Watching:

Adelaide and its surrounding regions are home to diverse ecosystems teeming with native wildlife, offering ample opportunities for wildlife enthusiasts to observe and appreciate Australia's unique fauna in their natural habitats. From koalas and kangaroos to dolphins and sea lions, there are countless species to encounter across Adelaide's parks, reserves, and coastal areas. Here are some recommended wildlife watching experiences near Adelaide:

1. Cleland Wildlife Park:
   - Description: Cleland Wildlife Park is a popular wildlife sanctuary located in the Adelaide Hills, offering visitors the opportunity to get up close and personal with a wide variety of native Australian animals in a natural bushland setting. Visitors can hand-feed kangaroos and wallabies, encounter koalas up close, and observe emus, wombats, echidnas, and native birds in their habitats. The park also offers guided tours, keeper talks, and wildlife encounters for a more immersive experience.
   - Website: [Cleland Wildlife Park] (https://www.environment.sa.gov.au/clelandwildlife)

2. Adelaide Dolphin Sanctuary:

- Description: The Adelaide Dolphin Sanctuary is a protected marine area located in the Port River estuary, home to a resident population of Indo-Pacific bottlenose dolphins. Visitors can embark on dolphin-spotting cruises or kayak tours to observe dolphins in their natural habitat, learn about their behavior and conservation, and enjoy scenic views of the mangrove-lined waterways. The sanctuary also supports a diverse range of birdlife, including pelicans, herons, and shorebirds.
   - Website: [Adelaide Dolphin Sanctuary] (https://www.adelaidekoicentre.com.au/)

3. Granite Island Recreation Park:
   - Description: Granite Island, located just off the coast of Victor Harbor, is a scenic island reserve known for its colony of Little Penguins (also known as Fairy Penguins). Visitors can take a leisurely stroll along the island's coastal walking trail, observing penguins, seabirds, and seals in their natural habitat. Guided penguin tours are available at dusk, offering the chance to see these adorable birds returning to their burrows after a day at sea.
   - Website: [Granite Island Recreation Park] (https://www.environment.sa.gov.au/parks/find-a-park/Browse_by_region/Fleurieu_Peninsula/granite-island-recreation-park)

4. Seal Bay Conservation Park:
   - Description: Seal Bay Conservation Park, located on Kangaroo Island, is home to one of the largest colonies of Australian sea lions in the world. Visitors can join guided tours to walk among these majestic marine mammals as they rest, play, and interact on the sandy shores of Seal Bay. The park offers a unique opportunity to observe sea lions in their natural habitat and learn about their behavior, biology, and conservation.
   - Website: [Seal Bay Conservation Park]

(https://www.environment.sa.gov.au/sealbay)

5. Morialta Conservation Park:
   - Description: Morialta Conservation Park, situated in the Adelaide foothills, is not only known for its scenic hiking trails and waterfalls but also for its abundant birdlife. Birdwatchers can spot a variety of native bird species, including rainbow lorikeets, honeyeaters, rosellas, and kookaburras, as well as elusive nocturnal birds such as owls and tawny frogmouths. The park's diverse habitats provide opportunities for birdwatching year-round.
   - Website: [Morialta Conservation Park] (https://www.environment.sa.gov.au/parks/find-a-park/Browse_by_region/Adelaide_Hills/morialta-conservation-park)

These wildlife watching experiences near Adelaide offer opportunities to connect with nature, observe fascinating animal behavior, and gain a deeper appreciation for Australia's rich biodiversity. Whether you're exploring bushland reserves, cruising along coastal waterways, or venturing to nearby islands, there's a wealth of wildlife to discover and enjoy in and around Adelaide.

9. Shopping

Rundle Mall:

Rundle Mall is Adelaide's premier shopping destination, offering a vibrant and diverse retail experience in the heart of the city. With its iconic pedestrian-friendly mall, historic arcades, department stores, boutiques, and specialty shops, Rundle Mall caters to shoppers of all tastes and budgets. Here's what you can expect when exploring Rundle Mall:

1. Retail Stores:
   - Description: Rundle Mall is home to a wide range of retail stores, from international brands and department stores to local boutiques and specialty shops. Whether you're shopping for fashion, accessories, electronics, homewares, or gifts, you'll find plenty of options to browse and explore.
   - Website: [Rundle Mall Retailers] (https://rundlemall.com/)

2. Rundle Mall Plaza:
   - Description: Rundle Mall Plaza is a multi-level shopping center located within Rundle Mall, offering a diverse selection of stores, cafes, and dining options. The plaza features major retailers, fashion boutiques, beauty salons, and specialty shops, providing a convenient and modern shopping experience in the heart of the city.
   - Website: [Rundle Mall Plaza] (https://rundlemall.com/shopping/rundle-mall-plaza/)

3. Arcades and Precincts:
   - Description: Rundle Mall is lined with historic arcades and precincts that add charm and character to the

shopping experience. Explore Adelaide Arcade, one of the city's oldest shopping arcades, featuring Victorian architecture and a mix of specialty stores and cafes. Venture into Regent Arcade, home to unique boutiques, jewelry stores, and gourmet food outlets. Don't miss the stylish Gays Arcade and the vibrant Adelaide Central Plaza, each offering its own selection of shops and services.
   - Websites:
 [Adelaide Arcade] (https://www.adelaidearcade.com.au/),
 [Regent Arcade] (https://www.regentarcade.com.au/),
 [Gays Arcade] (https://www.gaysarcade.com.au/),
 [Adelaide Central Plaza] (https://www.adelaidecentralplaza.com.au/)

4. Dining and Entertainment:
   - Description: Rundle Mall is not just a shopping destination but also a hub for dining and entertainment. Discover a variety of cafes, restaurants, and eateries offering cuisines from around the world, as well as food courts and takeaway options for quick bites on the go. Enjoy street performances, live music, and cultural events that add to the vibrant atmosphere of the mall.
   - Website: [Rundle Mall Dining] (https://rundlemall.com/eat-drink/)

5. Events and Promotions:
   - Description: Throughout the year, Rundle Mall hosts a calendar of events, promotions, and activities that attract shoppers and visitors from near and far. From seasonal sales and fashion shows to food festivals and live performances, there's always something happening in Rundle Mall to make your shopping experience even more enjoyable.

- Website: [Rundle Mall Events] (https://rundlemall.com/events/)

Rundle Mall offers a dynamic and bustling shopping experience that combines the best of retail, dining, entertainment, and culture, making it a must-visit destination for locals and tourists alike. Whether you're hunting for the latest fashion trends, searching for unique gifts, or simply soaking up the atmosphere, Rundle Mall has something for everyone to enjoy.

Boutique Stores:

In addition to the mainstream retailers and department stores, Rundle Mall and its surrounding areas are dotted with charming boutique stores offering unique and eclectic finds for shoppers seeking something distinctive and special. From fashion-forward clothing and accessories to artisanal homewares and gifts, these boutique stores add a touch of individuality and style to Adelaide's shopping scene. Here are some boutique stores you can explore in and around Rundle Mall:

1. Ginger:
   - Description: Ginger is a boutique store located in Rundle Mall Plaza, offering a curated selection of women's fashion, accessories, and gifts sourced from local and international designers. From stylish clothing and statement jewelry to handcrafted leather goods and homewares, Ginger showcases a mix of contemporary and timeless pieces for the modern woman.
   - Website: [Ginger](https://gingeronline.com.au/)

2. Naomi Murrell Studio Store:

- Description: The Naomi Murrell Studio Store, situated in the heart of Rundle Mall, is a haven for lovers of minimalist design and playful aesthetics. The store features a range of Australian-made clothing, jewelry, accessories, and lifestyle products designed by Naomi Murrell, known for her whimsical prints, bold colors, and timeless silhouettes.
   - Website: [Naomi Murrell] (https://naomimurrell.com/)

3. One Rundle Trading Co.:
   - Description: One Rundle Trading Co. is a boutique store located in Kent Town, just a short distance from Rundle Mall, offering a unique mix of fashion, homewares, and gifts with a vintage-inspired aesthetic. The store showcases an eclectic collection of clothing, footwear, accessories, and home decor items sourced from local and international designers, as well as vintage finds and one-of-a-kind treasures.
   - Website: [One Rundle Trading Co.] (https://onerundle.com.au/)

4. Miss Gladys Sym Choon:
   - Description: Miss Gladys Sym Choon is an iconic boutique store located on Rundle Street in the East End, offering a curated selection of fashion-forward clothing, accessories, and lifestyle products for men and women. The store features a mix of Australian and international labels, as well as emerging designers, with an emphasis on quality craftsmanship, unique design, and individual style.
   - Website: [Miss Gladys Sym Choon] (https://www.missgladyssymchoon.com.au/)

5. Urban Cow Studio:
   - Description: Urban Cow Studio is a vibrant artist-run gallery and boutique store located on Vaughan Place, just

off Rundle Street, showcasing the work of local artists, designers, and craftspeople. The store offers a diverse range of handmade and locally-produced artworks, prints, jewelry, ceramics, textiles, and homewares, providing a platform for emerging creatives to showcase their talent and creativity.
   - Website: [Urban Cow Studio] (https://www.urbancow.com.au/)

These boutique stores in and around Rundle Mall offer shoppers a unique shopping experience, with carefully curated collections, personalized service, and a focus on quality, craftsmanship, and individuality. Whether you're searching for the perfect outfit, a special gift, or a piece of art to treasure, you'll find something to delight and inspire at these boutique destinations in Adelaide.

Souvenir Shops:

For visitors looking to take home a piece of Adelaide's charm and character, there are several souvenir shops scattered throughout the city center, offering a delightful array of locally-made products, unique gifts, and iconic mementos that capture the spirit of South Australia. From Aboriginal artwork and gourmet treats to handmade crafts and Kangaroo Island specialties, these souvenir shops provide a treasure trove of keepsakes to commemorate your time in Adelaide. Here are some souvenir shops you can explore:

1. Hahndorf Souvenir & Gift Shop:
   - Description: Located in the historic German village of Hahndorf in the Adelaide Hills, the Hahndorf Souvenir & Gift Shop offers a wide selection of souvenirs, gifts, and local products celebrating the heritage and culture of South

Australia. Visitors can browse an assortment of Australian-made gifts, including Aboriginal art, handcrafted wooden items, gourmet food products, and traditional German souvenirs.

   - Location: 47 Main St, Hahndorf SA 5245
   - Website: [Hahndorf Souvenir & Gift Shop](https://hahndorfsouvenirshop.com.au/)

2. South Australian Museum Shop:

   - Description: The South Australian Museum Shop, located within the South Australian Museum in Adelaide's cultural precinct, offers a diverse range of souvenirs, books, and gifts inspired by the museum's exhibitions and collections. Visitors can discover an assortment of educational toys, indigenous crafts, jewelry, and natural history-inspired products, as well as books on South Australian culture, history, and wildlife.
   - Location: North Terrace, Adelaide SA 5000
   - Website: [South Australian Museum Shop](https://www.samuseum.sa.gov.au/shop)

3. Adelaide Central Market Souvenir Stalls:

   - Description: The Adelaide Central Market, located in the heart of the city, is a bustling marketplace renowned for its fresh produce, gourmet delights, and multicultural atmosphere. Within the market, visitors can find several souvenir stalls offering a variety of South Australian-themed gifts, including locally-made food products, artisanal crafts, Aboriginal art, and Kangaroo Island specialties such as honey, wines, and skincare products.
   - Location: 44-60 Gouger St, Adelaide SA 5000
   - Website: [Adelaide Central Market](https://adelaidecentralmarket.com.au/)

4. Adelaide Arcade Souvenir Shops:

- Description: Adelaide Arcade, one of the city's oldest shopping arcades, is home to several souvenir shops and specialty stores offering unique gifts, trinkets, and memorabilia. Visitors can explore a selection of South Australian-themed souvenirs, including postcards, keychains, magnets, tea towels, and plush toys, as well as handmade crafts, jewelry, and Aboriginal art.
   - Location: 112-118 Grenfell St, Adelaide SA 5000
   - Website: [Adelaide Arcade](https://www.adelaidearcade.com.au/)

5. Glenelg Beachfront Souvenir Shops:
   - Description: The seaside suburb of Glenelg, located just a short tram ride from Adelaide's city center, is home to a strip of souvenir shops along the bustling beachfront esplanade. Visitors can browse a range of beach-themed souvenirs, swimwear, sunscreen, and seaside accessories, as well as local artwork, crafts, and gifts inspired by the coastal lifestyle.
   - Location: Jetty Rd, Glenelg SA 5045

These souvenir shops offer a delightful selection of mementos and gifts that capture the essence of Adelaide and South Australia, providing visitors with cherished reminders of their time spent exploring the city's attractions, landmarks, and cultural treasures. Whether you're searching for traditional keepsakes, indigenous artworks, or gourmet treats, you're sure to find something special to take home from these souvenir destinations in Adelaide.

Local Markets:

Adelaide is home to a vibrant array of local markets, offering a diverse range of products, fresh produce, artisanal goods, and unique finds sourced from local producers, artisans, and small businesses. From bustling farmers' markets and artisan markets to eclectic flea markets and night markets, there's a market to suit every taste and interest in and around Adelaide. Here are some local markets you can explore:

1. Adelaide Central Market:
   - Description: The Adelaide Central Market is a bustling marketplace located in the heart of the city, offering an eclectic mix of fresh produce, gourmet delights, specialty foods, and artisanal products sourced from local growers, producers, and traders. With over 80 stalls selling everything from fruit and vegetables to cheese, meats, seafood, baked goods, and international delicacies, the market is a food lover's paradise and a vibrant hub of activity.
   - Location: 44-60 Gouger St, Adelaide SA 5000
   - Website: [Adelaide Central Market](https://adelaidecentralmarket.com.au/)

2. Glenelg Sunset Market:
   - Description: The Glenelg Sunset Market is a popular beachfront market held along the picturesque foreshore of Glenelg every Thursday evening during the summer months. Visitors can browse a variety of stalls selling handmade crafts, artisanal products, fashion accessories, jewelry, homewares, and gourmet food items, while enjoying live music, entertainment, and stunning sunset views over the Gulf St Vincent.
   - Location: Glenelg Foreshore, Glenelg SA 5045
   - Website: [Glenelg Sunset Market](https://www.glenelgsunsetmarkets.com.au/)

3. Adelaide Showground Farmers' Market:

- Description: The Adelaide Showground Farmers' Market is a weekly market held at the Adelaide Showground, showcasing a wide range of fresh, seasonal produce direct from local farmers, growers, and artisan producers. Visitors can shop for farm-fresh fruit and vegetables, organic meats, free-range eggs, artisan bread, cheese, olive oil, honey, preserves, and more, while supporting local agriculture and sustainable food production practices.
   - Location: Adelaide Showground, Goodwood Rd, Wayville SA 5034
   - Website: [Adelaide Showground Farmers' Market] (https://adelaidefarmersmarket.com.au/)

4. **Prospect Farmers' Market**:
   - Description: The Prospect Farmers' Market is a vibrant community market held on the second Sunday of each month at the Prospect Town Hall, showcasing a diverse range of fresh produce, gourmet foods, artisanal products, and handmade crafts from local vendors and producers. Visitors can explore stalls offering seasonal fruit and vegetables, organic meats, baked goods, coffee, wine, flowers, and more, while enjoying live music and family-friendly activities.
   - Location: Prospect Town Hall, 128 Prospect Rd, Prospect SA 5082
   - Website: [Prospect Farmers' Market] (https://www.prospect.sa.gov.au/explore/prospect-farmers-market)

5. **Adelaide Night Market**:
   - Description: The Adelaide Night Market is a vibrant night market held on selected Friday nights at the Adelaide Showground, featuring a lively atmosphere, street food vendors, artisan stalls, live music, entertainment, and family-friendly activities. Visitors can sample a variety of

international cuisines, browse stalls selling handmade crafts, fashion accessories, artwork, and gifts, and enjoy the bustling ambiance of this popular nocturnal market.

   - Location: Adelaide Showground, Goodwood Rd, Wayville SA 5034
   - Website: [Adelaide Night Market] (https://adelaidenightmarket.com.au/)

These local markets offer a diverse and dynamic shopping experience, providing visitors with the opportunity to discover unique products, support local businesses, and immerse themselves in Adelaide's vibrant market culture. Whether you're shopping for fresh produce, handmade crafts, gourmet treats, or souvenirs, you'll find plenty to explore and enjoy at these bustling marketplaces in and around Adelaide.

10. Nightlife and Entertainment

Bars and Pubs:

Adelaide's nightlife scene offers a diverse array of bars and pubs catering to every taste, from cozy neighborhood pubs and trendy cocktail bars to rooftop lounges and live music venues. Whether you're in the mood for craft cocktails, local brews, or a lively atmosphere, there's a bar or pub to suit your preferences. Here are some notable establishments to check out:

1. Clever Little Tailor:
   - Description: Clever Little Tailor is a stylish and intimate bar located in Adelaide's East End, known for its expertly crafted cocktails, extensive whiskey selection, and relaxed ambiance. The bar features a rotating menu of innovative cocktails made with premium spirits and house-made syrups, as well as a curated selection of local and international wines and craft beers.
   - Location: 19 Peel St, Adelaide SA 5000
   - Website: [Clever Little Tailor] (https://www.cleverlittletailor.com.au/)

2. Bank Street Social:
   - Description: Bank Street Social is a popular laneway bar nestled in the heart of Adelaide's CBD, offering a cozy and inviting atmosphere perfect for casual drinks and socializing. The bar boasts an extensive selection of craft beers on tap, creative cocktails, and boutique wines, as well as a menu of gourmet bar snacks and share plates.
   - Location: 48 Hindley St, Adelaide SA 5000
   - Website: [Bank Street Social] (https://www.bankstreetsocial.com.au/)

3. The Collins Bar:
   - Description: The Collins Bar is an elegant cocktail lounge located within the Hilton Adelaide hotel, renowned for its sophisticated atmosphere, creative libations, and impeccable service. The bar offers an extensive menu of classic and contemporary cocktails crafted with premium spirits, as well as a curated selection of fine wines, champagne, and spirits.
   - Location: 233 Victoria Square, Adelaide SA 5000
   - Website: [The Collins Bar] (https://www.hilton.com/en/hotels/adlhigi-hilton-adelaide/dining/the-collins-bar/)

4. Pink Moon Saloon:
   - Description: Pink Moon Saloon is a unique and quirky bar nestled in a laneway in Adelaide's West End, known for its rustic charm, cozy atmosphere, and creative cocktails. The bar is housed in a historic cottage and features a timber-clad interior, outdoor courtyard, and rooftop terrace, offering a laid-back setting to enjoy innovative drinks and delicious bar snacks.
   - Location: 21 Leigh St, Adelaide SA 5000
   - Website: [Pink Moon Saloon] (https://www.pinkmoonsaloon.com.au/)

5. The Austral Hotel:
   - Description: The Austral Hotel is a beloved heritage pub located in the heart of Adelaide's CBD, offering a lively atmosphere, friendly service, and a wide selection of beers on tap. The pub features multiple bars and dining areas, including a rooftop beer garden, sports bar, and live music venue, making it a popular destination for locals and visitors alike.
   - Location: 205 Rundle St, Adelaide SA 5000

- Website: [The Austral Hotel] (https://www.australhotel.com.au/)

These bars and pubs are just a taste of Adelaide's vibrant nightlife scene, where you can unwind with a drink, socialize with friends, and experience the city's unique hospitality and culture. Whether you're seeking craft cocktails, local brews, or live entertainment, you'll find plenty of options to enjoy a memorable night out in Adelaide.

Nightclubs:

Adelaide's nightlife comes alive after dark, with a variety of nightclubs offering pulsating beats, energetic dance floors, and unforgettable party experiences. Whether you're into electronic dance music, hip-hop, R&B, or top 40 hits, there's a nightclub to suit your music preferences and dancing style. Here are some of Adelaide's top nightclubs to check out:

1. HQ Complex:
   - Description: HQ Complex is Adelaide's largest and most iconic nightclub, known for its impressive sound system, state-of-the-art lighting, and electrifying atmosphere. The venue hosts a diverse range of events and club nights, featuring top DJs, live performances, and themed parties spanning genres such as EDM, house, techno, and more.
   - Location: 149 Hindley St, Adelaide SA 5000
   - Website: [HQ Complex] (https://hqcomplex.com.au/)

2. Red Square:
   - Description: Red Square is a premier nightclub located in Adelaide's East End, renowned for its stylish décor, VIP

booths, and high-energy dance floor. The club features a mix of resident and guest DJs spinning the latest hits, hip-hop, R&B, and electronic beats, creating a vibrant and dynamic atmosphere for partygoers to dance the night away.

   - Location: 111 Hindley St, Adelaide SA 5000
   - Website: [Red Square] (https://www.redsquare.com.au/)

3. Dog & Duck:
   - Description: The Dog & Duck is a popular nightclub and pub located in Adelaide's CBD, offering a lively atmosphere, affordable drinks, and regular DJ nights. The venue features multiple bars, pool tables, and a spacious dance floor, making it a favorite destination for locals and students looking to let loose and have fun.
   - Location: 161 Hindley St, Adelaide SA 5000
   - Website: [Dog & Duck] (https://dogandduck.com.au/)

4. The Grand Bar:
   - Description: The Grand Bar is a sophisticated nightclub and cocktail lounge situated in the historic Grand Hotel on North Terrace, offering a luxurious setting for a night out on the town. The venue features elegant décor, premium drinks, and a diverse music lineup, with resident DJs spinning a mix of chart-toppers, house music, and old-school classics.
   - Location: 55 North Terrace, Adelaide SA 5000
   - Website: [The Grand Bar] (https://www.grandbar.com.au/)

5. Rocket Bar & Rooftop:

- Description: Rocket Bar & Rooftop is a trendy nightclub and rooftop bar located in Adelaide's West End, known for its eclectic music, creative cocktails, and laid-back vibe. The venue hosts regular club nights and live music events, showcasing local and international talent across genres such as indie, rock, alternative, and electronic music.
   - Location: 142 Hindley St, Adelaide SA 5000
   - Website: [Rocket Bar & Rooftop] (https://www.rocketrooftop.com.au/)

These nightclubs offer an exhilarating nightlife experience, with pumping music, stylish venues, and energetic crowds ready to dance the night away. Whether you're celebrating a special occasion, letting loose with friends, or simply enjoying a night out on the town, you're sure to find an unforgettable party atmosphere at Adelaide's top nightclubs.

Live Music Venues:

Adelaide has a thriving live music scene, with a variety of venues showcasing talented local bands, emerging artists, and renowned musicians across a range of genres. From intimate bars and cozy pubs to larger concert halls and outdoor amphitheaters, there's a live music venue to suit every taste and mood. Here are some notable live music venues in Adelaide:

1. The Gov:
   - Description: The Governor Hindmarsh Hotel, known affectionately as "The Gov," is an iconic live music venue located in the suburb of Hindmarsh, just outside Adelaide's city center. The venue hosts a diverse range of live music performances, including concerts, gigs, and shows spanning genres such as rock, indie, blues, folk, and more.

With its intimate atmosphere, historic charm, and stellar lineup of local and international acts, The Gov is a must-visit destination for music lovers.
   - Location: 59 Port Rd, Hindmarsh SA 5007
   - Website: [The Gov](https://thegov.com.au/)

2. Thebarton Theatre:
   - Description: The Thebarton Theatre, also known as "Thebby," is a historic live music venue located in the suburb of Torrensville, renowned for its stunning art deco architecture and impressive acoustics. The venue hosts a wide range of live music events, including concerts, gigs, comedy shows, and theatrical performances, featuring both local and touring artists across various genres.
   - Location: 112 Henley Beach Rd, Torrensville SA 5031
   - Website: [Thebarton Theatre](https://thebartontheatre.com.au/)

3. Lion Arts Factory:
   - Description: Lion Arts Factory is a dynamic live music venue and cultural hub located in the West End of Adelaide, housed within the historic Lion Arts Centre. The venue showcases a diverse lineup of live music acts, including bands, DJs, solo artists, and performers across genres such as rock, indie, electronic, hip-hop, and more. With its industrial-chic aesthetic, intimate setting, and commitment to supporting local talent, Lion Arts Factory offers an immersive and memorable live music experience.
   - Location: 68 North Terrace, Adelaide SA 5000
   - Website: [Lion Arts Factory](https://www.lionartsfactory.com.au/)

4. The Jade:
   - Description: The Jade is a unique live music venue and cultural space located in the Adelaide suburb of Flinders Park, housed within a historic heritage building. The venue

hosts an eclectic array of live music performances, including gigs, concerts, open mic nights, and music festivals, showcasing local bands, solo artists, and alternative acts across genres such as folk, jazz, blues, and world music. With its intimate setting, relaxed atmosphere, and diverse programming, The Jade offers an inclusive and welcoming space for music enthusiasts and creatives.

   - Location: 160 Flinders St, Adelaide SA 5000
   - Website: [The Jade] (https://www.thejadeadl.com.au/)

5. The Wheatsheaf Hotel:
   - Description: The Wheatsheaf Hotel is a beloved live music venue and pub located in the suburb of Thebarton, known for its welcoming atmosphere, craft beer selection, and eclectic music lineup. The venue hosts regular live music performances, including gigs, concerts, and jam sessions, featuring local bands, solo artists, and touring acts across genres such as folk, blues, country, and acoustic music. With its intimate stage, laid-back vibe, and community-oriented ethos, The Wheatsheaf Hotel offers a relaxed and authentic live music experience for patrons of all ages.

   - Location: 39 George St, Thebarton SA 5031
   - Website: [The Wheatsheaf Hotel] (https://wheatsheafhotel.com.au/)

These live music venues showcase the vibrant and diverse music scene in Adelaide, providing music lovers with the opportunity to discover new artists, enjoy live performances, and immerse themselves in the city's rich musical culture. Whether you're into rock, indie, jazz, blues, or electronic music, you'll find plenty of talent and excitement at Adelaide's top live music venues.

Theatre Shows:

Adelaide boasts a vibrant theatre scene, with a variety of venues showcasing a diverse range of theatrical productions, from classic plays and musicals to contemporary dramas and experimental performances. Whether you're a fan of Broadway-style shows, thought-provoking dramas, or avant-garde theater, there's something for everyone to enjoy in Adelaide's thriving theatre community. Here are some notable venues where you can catch theatre shows:

1. Adelaide Festival Centre:
   - Description: The Adelaide Festival Centre is the premier performing arts venue in South Australia, hosting a wide range of theatre productions, musicals, dance performances, concerts, and cultural events throughout the year. The center comprises several theaters, including the Festival Theatre, Dunstan Playhouse, and Space Theatre, each offering a unique atmosphere and program of shows catering to diverse tastes and interests.
   - Location: King William Rd, Adelaide SA 5000
   - Website: [Adelaide Festival Centre] (https://www.adelaidefestivalcentre.com.au/)

2. Her Majesty's Theatre:
   - Description: Her Majesty's Theatre is a historic theater located in the heart of Adelaide's CBD, known for its grand Victorian architecture, elegant interiors, and rich theatrical heritage. The theater hosts a variety of theatrical productions, including musicals, plays, opera, ballet, and comedy shows, featuring both local and touring productions from around the world.
   - Location: 58 Grote St, Adelaide SA 5000
   - Website: [Her Majesty's Theatre]

(https://www.adelaidefestivalcentre.com.au/venues/her-majestys-theatre/)

3. The Space Theatre:
   - Description: The Space Theatre is a contemporary performance venue located within the Adelaide Festival Centre, specializing in intimate and innovative theatrical productions, experimental works, and cutting-edge performances. The theater showcases a diverse range of shows, including contemporary dramas, devised theater, physical theater, and multimedia performances, providing a platform for emerging artists and boundary-pushing works.
   - Location: King William Rd, Adelaide SA 5000
   - Website: [The Space Theatre] (https://www.adelaidefestivalcentre.com.au/venues/space-theatre/)

4. The Bakehouse Theatre:
   - Description: The Bakehouse Theatre is an independent performance venue located in the suburb of Adelaide, dedicated to supporting and showcasing local theater companies, emerging artists, and new works. The theater hosts a diverse program of productions, including plays, cabaret, comedy, and fringe performances, fostering a vibrant and inclusive arts community in Adelaide.
   - Location: 255 Angas St, Adelaide SA 5000
   - Website: [The Bakehouse Theatre] (https://www.bakehousetheatre.com/)

5. The Dunstan Playhouse:
   - Description: The Dunstan Playhouse is a versatile theater space located within the Adelaide Festival Centre, known for its contemporary design, flexible seating arrangements, and high-quality productions. The theater hosts a range of theatrical works, including classic plays,

modern dramas, musicals, and experimental performances, presented by local and touring theater companies.
   - Location: King William Rd, Adelaide SA 5000
   - Website: [The Dunstan Playhouse] (https://www.adelaidefestivalcentre.com.au/venues/dunstan-playhouse/)

These theater venues offer a rich and diverse program of theatrical productions, providing audiences with the opportunity to experience world-class performances, discover new works, and engage with the vibrant arts scene in Adelaide. Whether you're a theater enthusiast, a casual theatergoer, or someone looking for a memorable night out, you'll find plenty to enjoy at Adelaide's top theatre venues.

11. Day Trips and Excursions

McLaren Vale Wine Region:

Embark on a delightful day trip to the picturesque McLaren Vale Wine Region, located just a short drive south of Adelaide. Renowned for its stunning landscapes, award-winning wineries, and gourmet food offerings, McLaren Vale promises an unforgettable experience for wine enthusiasts and foodies alike. Here's what you can expect during your day trip to McLaren Vale:

- **Winery Tours and Tastings:**
  Indulge in a wine tasting adventure as you explore the acclaimed wineries of McLaren Vale. With over 80 cellar doors to choose from, you'll have the opportunity to sample a diverse range of wines, from world-class Shiraz and Cabernet Sauvignon to elegant Chardonnay and Grenache. Join guided tours of boutique wineries, chat with passionate winemakers, and savor the flavors of McLaren Vale's premium wine offerings.

- **Gourmet Dining**:
  Treat your taste buds to a culinary journey through McLaren Vale's gourmet food scene. Many wineries in the region boast onsite restaurants and cafes, serving up fresh, locally sourced cuisine paired perfectly with their wines. From casual lunches overlooking vineyards to fine dining experiences showcasing seasonal produce and regional flavors, McLaren Vale offers a wealth of dining options to suit every palate.

- **Scenic Vineyard Views**:
  Take in the breathtaking beauty of McLaren Vale's rolling hills, vineyards, and coastal vistas as you explore the

region's scenic countryside. Drive along picturesque routes lined with grapevines, stop at lookout points for panoramic views of the landscape, and capture memorable moments amidst the idyllic setting of South Australia's premier wine region.

- Artisan Producers and Farm Gates:
Discover the artisanal delights of McLaren Vale beyond wine, with visits to local producers, farm gates, and gourmet food stores. Sample handmade cheeses, olive oils, chocolates, and other artisanal products crafted with care by passionate producers using locally sourced ingredients. Stock up on culinary souvenirs to bring a taste of McLaren Vale home with you.

- Outdoor Activities and Nature Trails:
Immerse yourself in McLaren Vale's natural beauty with outdoor activities and nature trails perfect for exploring the region's diverse landscapes. Go for a leisurely stroll through vineyards and olive groves, embark on a scenic bike ride along dedicated trails, or venture into nearby conservation parks for bushwalking, birdwatching, and wildlife encounters.

- Cultural Attractions and Events:
Experience the vibrant culture of McLaren Vale through its arts, music, and community events. Check out art galleries showcasing local talent, attend live music performances at wineries and venues, or join in on special events such as food and wine festivals, harvest celebrations, and cultural gatherings that showcase the region's rich heritage and creative spirit.

A day trip to McLaren Vale offers a perfect blend of wine, food, nature, and culture, providing a memorable escape from the city and an opportunity to indulge in the best that South Australia has to offer. Whether you're a wine aficionado, a food lover, or simply seeking a scenic retreat, McLaren Vale promises a day of discovery and delight amidst the beauty of its wine country landscape.

Adelaide Hills Wineries:

Embark on a delightful day trip to the Adelaide Hills, a picturesque region just a short drive from Adelaide known for its cool climate wines, stunning landscapes, and charming cellar doors. Explore the rolling hills, verdant vineyards, and quaint towns of the Adelaide Hills as you discover some of the region's finest wineries and indulge in wine tastings, gourmet food experiences, and scenic vistas. Here's what you can expect during your day trip to Adelaide Hills wineries:

- **Wine Tastings and Cellar Door Experiences:**
Venture to the Adelaide Hills' acclaimed wineries and cellar doors to sample a diverse range of cool climate wines, including elegant Chardonnay, aromatic Sauvignon Blanc, and vibrant Pinot Noir. Chat with knowledgeable winemakers, learn about the winemaking process, and savor the flavors of handcrafted wines produced with passion and expertise. From boutique family-owned vineyards to larger estates with stunning views, Adelaide Hills offers a variety of wine tasting experiences to suit every palate.

- **Scenic Vineyard Views and Picnic Spots:**
Enjoy breathtaking vistas of rolling vineyards, lush countryside, and distant mountain ranges as you explore

the Adelaide Hills wine region. Many wineries offer picturesque picnic spots where you can relax with a glass of wine and a gourmet picnic basket filled with locally sourced delights. Take in the serenity of the landscape, breathe in the fresh mountain air, and soak up the beauty of nature surrounding you.

- Farm-to-Table Dining and Culinary Experiences:
   Treat yourself to farm-fresh cuisine and gourmet dining experiences at the Adelaide Hills' acclaimed winery restaurants and cafes. Indulge in seasonal menus showcasing locally sourced produce, artisanal cheeses, and handcrafted delicacies paired perfectly with the region's cool climate wines. From casual lunches on sunny terraces to fine dining experiences in elegant dining rooms, Adelaide Hills offers a wealth of culinary delights to tantalize your taste buds.

- Artisanal Producers and Food Trails:
   Discover the artisanal delights of the Adelaide Hills beyond wine, with visits to local producers, farm gates, and food trails. Sample handcrafted cheeses, artisan chocolates, gourmet preserves, and other regional specialties crafted with care by passionate producers. Explore the Adelaide Hills' food and wine trails, stopping at roadside stalls, farmers' markets, and artisanal shops to taste the best of the region's culinary offerings.

- Historic Towns and Cultural Attractions:
   Explore the charming towns and historic villages dotted throughout the Adelaide Hills, each with its own unique character and attractions. Stroll through tree-lined streets lined with heritage buildings, browse boutique shops showcasing local crafts and artwork, and immerse yourself in the region's rich history and cultural heritage. Visit art

galleries, museums, and cultural centers to learn about the Adelaide Hills' fascinating past and vibrant arts scene.

A day trip to the Adelaide Hills wineries offers a perfect blend of wine, food, nature, and culture, providing a memorable escape from the city and an opportunity to experience the best of South Australia's cool climate wine country. Whether you're a wine connoisseur, a foodie, or a nature lover, Adelaide Hills promises a day of discovery and delight amidst the beauty of its scenic landscapes and renowned wine region.

Kangaroo Island:

Escape to the pristine wilderness and breathtaking beauty of Kangaroo Island on an unforgettable day trip from Adelaide. Located just a short ferry ride or scenic flight from the mainland, Kangaroo Island boasts stunning landscapes, abundant wildlife, and a wealth of natural attractions waiting to be explored. Whether you're seeking wildlife encounters, coastal adventures, or simply a day of relaxation in nature, Kangaroo Island offers a diverse range of experiences to suit every traveler. Here's what you can expect during your day trip to Kangaroo Island:

- Wildlife Encounters:
Experience close encounters with Australia's iconic wildlife as you explore the natural habitats of Kangaroo Island. Encounter kangaroos, wallabies, and echidnas in their natural environment, observe playful seals basking on rocky shores, and marvel at the diverse birdlife, including pelicans, penguins, and colorful parrots. Visit wildlife sanctuaries, conservation parks, and pristine beaches for unforgettable wildlife viewing opportunities.

- **Natural Wonders and Scenic Landscapes:**
Immerse yourself in Kangaroo Island's stunning natural beauty as you discover its diverse landscapes, from rugged coastlines and pristine beaches to dense forests and rolling hills. Explore iconic landmarks such as Remarkable Rocks, Admiral's Arch, and Seal Bay Conservation Park, where you can witness the dramatic rock formations, sea cliffs, and coastal vistas that define the island's scenic allure.

- **Outdoor Adventures and Nature Trails**:
Embark on outdoor adventures and nature trails that showcase Kangaroo Island's rugged terrain and rich biodiversity. Hike through national parks and conservation reserves, follow coastal trails to hidden coves and secluded beaches, or embark on guided eco-tours and wildlife safaris led by knowledgeable local guides. From bushwalking and birdwatching to snorkeling and kayaking, there are plenty of outdoor activities to enjoy on Kangaroo Island.

- **Local Cuisine and Gourmet Delights**:
Savor the flavors of Kangaroo Island's gourmet produce and local cuisine as you dine at charming cafes, seaside eateries, and farmgate stalls showcasing the island's finest ingredients. Sample fresh seafood, artisanal cheeses, honey, olive oil, and premium wines produced by local farmers and producers, and indulge in delicious meals crafted with care and creativity using seasonal produce sourced from the island's abundant land and sea.

- **Cultural Experiences and Artisanal Crafts**:
Discover the rich cultural heritage and artistic talents of Kangaroo Island through visits to local galleries, studios, and artisan workshops. Meet talented artists and craftspeople, browse unique artworks, jewelry, and handcrafted souvenirs inspired by the island's natural beauty, and gain insight into the island's history, culture,

and community spirit through immersive cultural experiences and guided tours.

A day trip to Kangaroo Island offers a perfect blend of wildlife encounters, natural wonders, outdoor adventures, and culinary delights, providing a memorable escape to a pristine island paradise teeming with beauty and biodiversity. Whether you're seeking adventure, relaxation, or cultural immersion, Kangaroo Island promises a day of discovery and wonder amidst the splendor of its untouched wilderness and coastal landscapes.

Fleurieu Peninsula:

Embark on a scenic day trip to the Fleurieu Peninsula, a coastal paradise located just south of Adelaide. Known for its stunning beaches, picturesque landscapes, and charming seaside towns, the Fleurieu Peninsula offers a wealth of attractions and experiences for visitors to enjoy. Whether you're seeking outdoor adventures, gourmet delights, or cultural exploration, the Fleurieu Peninsula has something for everyone. Here's what you can expect during your day trip to the Fleurieu Peninsula:

- **Coastal Scenery and Beaches:**
   Discover the breathtaking beauty of the Fleurieu Peninsula's coastline as you explore its pristine beaches, rugged cliffs, and sparkling bays. From popular swimming and surfing spots to secluded coves and rocky outcrops, the peninsula boasts a variety of coastal landscapes waiting to be explored. Take a leisurely stroll along the shore, go for a dip in the crystal-clear waters, or simply relax and soak up the sun on the sandy shores of iconic beaches such as Port Willunga, Aldinga, and Victor Harbor.

- Wine Tasting and Cellar Doors:
Indulge in a wine tasting adventure as you tour the boutique wineries and cellar doors scattered throughout the Fleurieu Peninsula's picturesque wine regions. Sample a variety of premium wines, including Shiraz, Cabernet Sauvignon, and Sauvignon Blanc, crafted from the region's rich terroir and cool climate. Chat with passionate winemakers, learn about the winemaking process, and enjoy scenic vineyard views as you sip and savor the flavors of Fleurieu Peninsula wines.

- Culinary Experiences and Farm-to-Table Dining:
Treat your taste buds to the fresh flavors of the Fleurieu Peninsula's gourmet produce and farm-to-table cuisine. Visit local farmers' markets, artisanal food producers, and farm gates to sample delicious cheeses, olives, honey, and other regional specialties. Dine at acclaimed restaurants, cafes, and winery eateries serving seasonal menus featuring locally sourced ingredients, paired perfectly with the region's fine wines and craft beverages.

- Outdoor Adventures and Nature Trails:
Immerse yourself in the natural beauty of the Fleurieu Peninsula with outdoor adventures and nature trails suitable for all ages and fitness levels. Explore national parks, conservation reserves, and coastal trails offering scenic bushwalks, wildlife spotting, birdwatching, and picnicking opportunities. Embark on guided eco-tours, horseback riding adventures, or dolphin and whale watching cruises to experience the peninsula's diverse landscapes and marine life up close.

- Historic Towns and Cultural Attractions:
Discover the rich history and cultural heritage of the Fleurieu Peninsula as you explore its charming towns,

historic landmarks, and cultural attractions. Wander through heritage-listed streets lined with historic buildings, visit local museums, art galleries, and cultural centers to learn about the region's indigenous heritage, maritime history, and colonial past. Attend community events, festivals, and markets showcasing the vibrant arts, music, and culture of the Fleurieu Peninsula.

A day trip to the Fleurieu Peninsula offers a perfect blend of coastal beauty, culinary delights, outdoor adventures, and cultural exploration, providing a memorable escape to a region of natural wonders and seaside charm just a stone's throw from Adelaide. Whether you're seeking relaxation, adventure, or cultural immersion, the Fleurieu Peninsula promises a day of discovery and enjoyment amidst the splendor of its coastal landscapes and vibrant communities.

Murray River Cruises:

Experience the tranquility and beauty of the Murray River on a scenic day cruise, offering a relaxing escape into nature and a glimpse into the rich history and culture of Australia's longest river system. Departing from various locations along the river, Murray River cruises provide a leisurely journey through picturesque landscapes, charming riverside towns, and iconic landmarks, allowing passengers to unwind, explore, and immerse themselves in the river's natural splendor. Here's what you can expect during your day cruise on the Murray River:

- Scenic River Views and Natural Beauty:
Sit back, relax, and soak up the stunning scenery as you cruise along the Murray River, admiring its tranquil waters, lush riverbanks, and diverse wildlife. Enjoy

panoramic views of the surrounding landscapes, including towering gum trees, rugged cliffs, and fertile farmland, while listening to informative commentary from knowledgeable guides highlighting the river's ecology, history, and significance.

- Historic Paddle Steamers and Riverboats:
Step back in time aboard a historic paddle steamer or riverboat, offering a nostalgic journey along the Murray River reminiscent of the golden age of river travel. Marvel at the craftsmanship and engineering of these iconic vessels as they navigate the river's meandering course, powered by their distinctive paddle wheels. Learn about the role of paddle steamers in Australia's maritime history and hear fascinating stories of life on the river during the 19th and early 20th centuries.

- Riverside Towns and Attractions:
Discover charming riverside towns and attractions along the Murray River as you cruise past historic wharves, bustling river ports, and scenic landmarks. Stop at quaint riverfront villages such as Mannum, Renmark, and Echuca, where you can disembark to explore local attractions, heritage sites, and cultural landmarks, or simply wander through town, browsing shops, cafes, and galleries at your leisure.

- Wildlife Watching and Birdlife:
Keep your eyes peeled for native wildlife and birdlife along the Murray River, home to a diverse array of species inhabiting its banks, wetlands, and waterways. Spot kangaroos, emus, and koalas in their natural habitat, watch for playful dolphins and waterbirds frolicking in the river, and listen to the calls of native birds such as kookaburras, cockatoos, and lorikeets as they inhabit the riverine environment.

- Gourmet Dining and Onboard Entertainment:
Indulge in gourmet dining and onboard entertainment as you cruise the Murray River in style and comfort. Enjoy delicious meals featuring locally sourced produce and regional specialties served in elegant dining rooms or alfresco decks with panoramic views of the river. Take part in wine tastings, live music performances, and interactive activities showcasing the best of Murray River hospitality and entertainment.

A day cruise on the Murray River offers a perfect blend of relaxation, exploration, and immersion in nature, providing a memorable journey through one of Australia's most iconic waterways. Whether you're seeking adventure, history, or simply a peaceful retreat into nature, a Murray River cruise promises a day of serenity and discovery amidst the beauty of the Australian landscape and riverine environment.

Here are some contact details and websites for service providers in the mentioned regions:

McLaren Vale Wine Region:

1. McLaren Vale Grape Wine & Tourism Association:
   - Website: [mclarenvale.info] (https://mclarenvale.info/)
   - Contact: +61 8 8323 8999

2. d'Arenberg Winery:
   - Website: [darenberg.com.au] (https://www.darenberg.com.au/)
   - Contact: +61 8 8329 4888

3. Chapel Hill Winery:
   - Website: [chapelhillwine.com.au]

(https://www.chapelhillwine.com.au/)
   - Contact: +61 8 8323 8429

Adelaide Hills Wineries:

1. Adelaide Hills Wine Region:
   - Website: [adelaidehillswine.com.au] (https://www.adelaidehillswine.com.au/)
   - Contact: +61 8 8389 8339

2. Shaw + Smith Winery:
   - Website: [shawandsmith.com] (https://www.shawandsmith.com/)
   - Contact: +61 8 8398 0500

3. The Lane Vineyard:
   - Website: [thelane.com.au] (https://www.thelane.com.au/)
   - Contact: +61 8 8388 1250

Kangaroo Island:

1. Kangaroo Island Tourism:
   - Website: [tourkangarooisland.com.au] (https://www.tourkangarooisland.com.au/)
   - Contact: +61 8 8553 1185

2. Sealink Kangaroo Island Ferries:
   - Website: [sealink.com.au/kangaroo-island-ferry] (https://www.sealink.com.au/kangaroo-island-ferry/)
   - Contact: 131 301

3. Kangaroo Island Odysseys:
   - Website: [kangarooislandodysseys.com.au] (https://www.kangarooislandodysseys.com.au/)
   - Contact: +61 8 8553 0386

Fleurieu Peninsula:

1. Fleurieu Peninsula Tourism:
   - Website: [fleurieupeninsula.com.au] (https://www.fleurieupeninsula.com.au/)
   - Contact: +61 8 8556 5405

2. McLaren Vale Visitor Information Centre:
   - Website: [mclarenvale.info] (https://mclarenvale.info/)
   - Contact: +61 8 8323 9944

3. Victor Harbor Visitor Information Centre:
   - Website: [encountervictorharbor.com.au] (https://www.encountervictorharbor.com.au/)
   - Contact: +61 8 8551 0777

Murray River Cruises:

1. Murray River Paddlesteamers:
   - Website: [murrayriverpaddlesteamers.com.au] (https://www.murrayriverpaddlesteamers.com.au/)
   - Contact: +61 3 5482 5244

2. Captain Cook Cruises - Murray River:
   - Website: [captaincook.com.au/murray-river] (https://www.captaincook.com.au/murray-river/)
   - Contact: 1300 729 938

3. Murray River Cruises - Mannum:
   - Website: [murrayrivercruises.com.au] (https://www.murrayrivercruises.com.au/)
   - Contact: +61 8 8569 2544

These contact details and websites should help you plan your visit and book services for your desired experiences in each of these regions.

12. Practical Information

Currency and Banking:

- Currency: The currency used in Australia is the Australian Dollar (AUD). Notes come in denominations of $5, $10, $20, $50, and $100, while coins come in denominations of $2, $1, 50 cents, 20 cents, 10 cents, and 5 cents.

- Banking: Banks in Australia are typically open from Monday to Friday, with some branches offering limited hours on Saturdays. ATMs are widely available throughout cities and towns, allowing you to withdraw cash using international debit or credit cards.

Language:

- Language: English is the primary language spoken in Australia. However, due to its multicultural population, you may also encounter speakers of other languages, especially in urban areas.

Emergency Numbers:

- Emergency Services: In case of emergencies, dial 000 for police, fire, or ambulance services. This number is toll-free and can be accessed from any phone, including mobile phones.

Tourist Information Centers:

- Tourist Information Centers (TICs) can provide valuable assistance and resources for travelers. These centers offer maps, brochures, and advice on accommodation, attractions, and activities. Look for TICs in major cities, airports, and popular tourist destinations.

Tipping Customs:

- Tipping is not as common or expected in Australia as it is in some other countries. However, it is appreciated for exceptional service in restaurants, cafes, and bars, especially in upscale establishments. If you're satisfied with the service, you can leave a tip of around 10% of the total bill. Tipping for other services, such as taxi rides or hotel stays, is discretionary and not obligatory.

13. Travel Tips

Best Time to Visit:

- The best time to visit Adelaide and its surrounding regions, such as the McLaren Vale Wine Region and the Fleurieu Peninsula, is during the spring (September to November) and autumn (March to May) months. During these seasons, the weather is mild, and outdoor activities are enjoyable without the extreme heat of summer or the chill of winter.

Packing Essentials:

- Sunscreen: Protect yourself from the strong Australian sun with a high SPF sunscreen.
- Hat and Sunglasses: Shield your eyes and face from the sun's rays.
- Comfortable Shoes: Whether you're exploring the city streets or hiking in nature reserves, comfortable shoes are essential.
- Light Layers: Pack lightweight clothing suitable for layering to accommodate changes in temperature throughout the day.
- Insect Repellent: Especially important if you're venturing into bushland or near waterways.
- Reusable Water Bottle: Stay hydrated, especially during warmer months, by carrying a refillable water bottle.
- Travel Adapter: Australian power outlets use plugs with three flat pins, so make sure to bring a suitable adapter if your devices have different plugs.

Safety Tips:

- Swim Safely: Only swim in designated areas on beaches and always follow safety signs and lifeguard instructions.

- Stay Hydrated: Keep hydrated, especially during hot weather, by drinking plenty of water.
- Sun Protection: Wear sunscreen, hats, and sunglasses to protect yourself from the sun's UV rays.
- Emergency Contacts: Keep a list of emergency contacts, including local authorities and your country's embassy or consulate.

Etiquette and Customs:

- Respect Indigenous Culture: Acknowledge and respect the Indigenous heritage of the land by learning about local Aboriginal culture and customs.
- Queuing: Australians generally queue patiently in lines and appreciate the same courtesy from others.
- Tipping: While not obligatory, tipping for exceptional service in restaurants and bars is appreciated but not expected.

Useful Phrases:

- "G'day" - Hello
- "How are you going?" - How are you?
- "Cheers" - Thank you
- "No worries" - No problem
- "Good on ya" - Well done/Good job
- "Mate" - Friend/Companion
- "Ta" - Thanks

Learning a few basic phrases can go a long way in making your interactions with locals more enjoyable and respectful.

14. Resources

Maps:
- Google Maps: An excellent tool for navigating both urban areas and rural regions. Download offline maps for areas with limited internet connectivity.
- Tourist Information Centers: Visit local tourist information centers for free maps and brochures of the area.

Recommended Reading:
- Lonely Planet Guidebooks: Lonely Planet offers comprehensive guidebooks for various regions, including Adelaide and South Australia, providing insights into attractions, accommodations, dining, and more.
- Travel Blogs and Websites: Explore travel blogs and websites dedicated to Australia and South Australia for firsthand accounts, tips, and recommendations from fellow travelers.
- Local Literature: Immerse yourself in the culture and history of Adelaide and its surrounding regions by reading books and novels set in South Australia.

Online Resources:
- Official Tourism Websites: Visit official tourism websites for Adelaide, South Australia, and specific regions like the McLaren Vale Wine Region and Kangaroo Island for up-to-date information on attractions, events, accommodations, and travel tips.
- TripAdvisor: Browse traveler reviews, recommendations, and ratings for accommodations, restaurants, and attractions in Adelaide and its surrounding areas.
- Weather Forecast Websites: Check weather forecasts on websites like the Australian Bureau of Meteorology for the latest weather updates and forecasts for your travel dates.

Travel Apps:
- TripIt: Organize your travel plans, including flights, accommodations, and activities, in one place with TripIt. The app also provides itinerary management and real-time updates.
- XE Currency: Convert currencies and track exchange rates with XE Currency, useful for budgeting and managing expenses while traveling.
- Airbnb: Use the Airbnb app to find and book unique accommodations, from apartments and houses to villas and treehouses, in Adelaide and its surrounding regions.
- Uber or Lyft: Get around Adelaide and its suburbs conveniently with ridesharing apps like Uber or Lyft, offering affordable and reliable transportation options.

These resources will help you plan and navigate your trip to Adelaide and its surrounding regions, ensuring a smooth and enjoyable travel experience.

Map

Click the link or scan the QR code below to view map:

https://maps.app.goo.gl/ah6okn6bgVaogoCFA

Printed in Dunstable, United Kingdom